Oscar's

A+ Band Director Guide:
A Veteran Band Teacher's Guide to Teaching Music

Oscar Dames
oscarshorndames@gmail.com

ISBN: 978-976-96375-0-4 (print)
ISBN: 978-976-96375-1-1 (ebook)

Ordering Information:
Special discounts are available on quantity purchases by corporations, associations, and others. For details, contact 242-422-0593

Table of Contents

This book is dedicated first of all to God from whence cometh my strength, and to all my family, teachers, students, and friends who have contributed much to my musical journey thus far.

To my parents, Milton and Emily Dames, for making the sacrifice and enrolling me in private music lessons at a young age.

To my beautiful wife, Rachelle Dames, and to my sons, Oscar Jr., Ontario, and Othello who have been my pillar of strength and an inspiration for me to continue in this noble profession of music education.

I love you all, and I thank you for your continued support.

Oscar's

A+ Band Director Guide:
A Veteran Band Teacher's Guide to Teaching Music

Oscar Dames

Chapter 1:
New Teacher

Trained Teacher has been stamped across your certificate, and you have walked across the stage, shaken hands, flipped your tassel to the left, and after the official announcement, tossed your cap into the air as a demonstration of your achievement.

Now you begin a new journey of seeking employment and working in the capacity of a band director or music teacher. This book was written to assist new band directors or music teachers who have completed their certification or teacher training and are entering the teaching profession for the first time. By using the strategies discussed throughout this book, you will gain a wealth of knowledge and information that will set you up for a successful career as a band director or music teacher. This book is designed to give you a strong foundation on which to build your career, and you will learn how to function effectively in and out of the music classroom environment.

With over 30 years of experience as a musician working with young people, I have experimented with many strategies and implemented them in my classroom. They have proven to be successful, as manifested through the accomplishment of my students, many of whom are now established musicians.

These students are making their contribution throughout The Bahamas and also abroad. Some are in the teaching profession; others are performing in military bands such as the world-famous Royal Bahamas Police Force Band, the Royal Bahamas Defence Force Band, and the Department of Corrections Band; and others are leading and managing their private band.

The chapters of this book guide you chronologically through the important steps you need to take in order to develop a successful band or music program that advances your students and keeps you employed. Included in this book's Appendices are various sample forms that can be used to supplement your daily operating procedures. These forms can be adapted to your specific circumstances, thus eliminating the time you would have to spend creating new forms if your school does not have them in place.

Chapter 2:

Now That You Know Everything, Forget It

Yes, you have gone through your teaching practice, which was designed to give you a real-life working experience in an established education system. However, entering a school as a newly trained teacher can be a different experience for a number of reasons.

First, the training process for any career is always different from the real-life situation. Training is just to see if you have what it takes or can operate in a particular environment even if only at the minimum level. The situation always looks different when looking from the outside in. Once you are officially on the inside, it is usually not what you had expected.

The experience could be likened to when you were in high school and you couldn't wait to enter the job market, but when that opportunity came along, you wished you were still in school. In the same way, your teaching practice experience is a totally different experience from actually being employed with an institution. Reality sets in quickly and you have to start figuring out things for yourself in order to survive. This experience can be like stepping off a boat or a plane for the first time in a new country, and you have a very limited proficiency with the language.

Second, in teaching practice, you were probably assigned a supervisor and a teacher who was responsible for holding your hand and guiding you through the process. In an arrangement such as this, you were most likely given complete autonomy to design, arrange, and set up your classroom according to the guidelines laid out in your method courses and the institution's teaching practice manual. However, you may find that your new school has a different system in the way things are done.

The curriculum may be entirely different from the one you were trained in. A music teacher colleague of mine who just completed his Doctorate told me that he is teaching at a private school where the curriculum is totally different from the ones he is used to, and it sometimes has his head hurting. Similarly, you may find yourself in a school where you are not allowed to teach a particular topic, perform certain genres of music, or interact with students in a certain way.

Third, in your new school you may be fortunate to have an experienced teacher assigned to you as a mentor. Even in this case, you are looked upon as a trained teacher, and you will be expected to produce and accomplish the goals and objectives of the school. The mentor's role will be to provide technical and moral support and to guide you regarding the culture of the school—but not to do your work for you. Veteran musician Denis Donaldson, now deceased, once said, "It is not sufficient for a musician to go on stage and hold up a certificate; they have to perform." Achieving your teacher's certificate will only get you in the door; you are then required to execute your duties to the highest standard.

Fourth, you may be assigned to a grade level different from the ones you were trained to teach during your practice sessions. Teaching grades one and two, for example, is a different experience and requires different skills when compared to teaching grades five and six. The attention span of students in grades one and two will be shorter, and you will need to design more activities to keep them engaged. On the other hand, grades five and six students will be able to focus on an activity for a longer period. Also, in a new school, you may be called upon to teach a particular grade level or levels that you did not teach during teacher training due to various circumstances. It may be the only available position at the time, or you may be the only music teacher in the school, or you may end up in an all-age school or a special school.

Fifth, students tend to conduct themselves appropriately if and when they see the need to. During teaching practice, they may have been admonished by their regular teacher to cooperate with you, given that you were a teacher in training. In some cases, the behaviorally challenged students may have been pulled from your class and placed in another teacher's class. Also, for the most part, students tend to conduct themselves appropriately when they know that you are being evaluated by an external person. However, in a normal classroom setting, you will have to teach all the students, no matter how they are conducting themselves.

Teachers do not have the luxury, especially in the public school system, to choose who they want to teach. They have to work with the class list they are given by an administrator or their Head of Department. To make matters worse, during the sorting process students who are more academically inclined are placed on an academic track, such as Academic Science, Business, and Computer Science while the remainder of students are split between the Arts such as Performing Arts, Fine Arts, Culinary Arts, and Industrial Arts.

On more than one occasion, I have had students in music who were academically inclined and wanted to be in music but were coerced by another teacher to move to an academic program. One of those students decided after a week to transfer back because music was where his heart was. Now he is in college on a music scholarship.

Last, in the case of young teachers, students may try to take advantage of them because they feel that they are more or less in the same age range—as is usually the case in senior high schools. Some students may be 17, 18, or 19 while the teacher may be only a few years older; hence, these students may not see the teacher as an authority figure. Also, in some cases, a teacher may not be young but may appear young. In my capacity as Senior Master responsible for discipline, I have had, on more than one occasion, new female teachers report to me that male students were being familiar and conducting themselves inappropriately towards them.

Students may also tend to take advantage of teachers who are new to their school because they know they are not familiar with the environment, don't know the standard operating procedures, and don't know their way around.

Early in the school year, my school had a fire drill and there was a new teacher at the school who did not know the evacuation procedure, including the route and the designated meeting area. After the drill, I asked her how she managed with her class during the exercise. She said that she did not know the procedure so she had to take instructions from her students, who guided her and led the way to the evacuation site. This is an example of how students can influence the outcome of a situation, either in a positive or negative way, when you are a new teacher in a new environment.

It is important that you be aware of the fact that all institutions operate on a different system based on a number of variables.

If you are not already about to be hired by a specific institution, then your number one priority will likely be to seek employment. Therefore, the next chapter is designed to provide information that will help you successfully land the job at the prestigious institution where you seek employment.

Chapter 3

Get the Job You Want When You Want It

Your college or university should be one of the first places you reach out to when seeking employment. I obtained my Masters in Music Education degree from VanderCook College of Music in Chicago, which specializes in creating excellent music teachers. As a result, many schools contact the college when they are seeking to hire music teachers. I remain on the college's mailing list, and therefore I receive emails requesting teachers to apply for various positions. Hence, for you as a new teacher, contacting your college or university may be beneficial in terms of steering you in the right direction regarding employment.

Try to provide good examples and to do your best at all times because various people are looking up to you and, in this new age of technology, your story is there for all to see. Job recruiters and persons hiring will search the various social media platforms to find out information about you before you are considered for employment. Your relationship with people, and your past experiences, will play a significant role in you getting hired for a new teaching position.

Curriculum Vitae

A curriculum vitae, or resume, is required when you apply for any job, and you should have one ready at all times. At some point in your college or university life, you should have been required to generate your curriculum vitae. Having done so, you will only have to update it when the need arises. The curriculum vitae is your first step in the door, and it shows your potential employer that you have at least met the minimum requirements for the new job. The document will include contact information, previous employment, education status, and special skills, all in chronological order. It will be to your advantage to include all additional relevant information that can help to place you in a better position to get hired compared to your competitors.

References

While a curriculum vitae shows your skills and qualifications on paper, as outlined by you, a reference will speak on your behalf from another person's perspective. This is why, when applying for employment, you are required to submit references from several people who are familiar with your work. When you submit references, try to include persons who can speak to various aspects of your life, for example: You as a student, you as an employee, you as a community builder, you as a lifelong learner, and you as someone who works well with other people. References should be seen to be genuine and not biased; therefore, do not submit references from family members.

Original Documents

You will need to submit your documents when they are requested. Ensure that all of your original documents are kept together in a safe place so they are readily accessible when the time comes to submit them. Official college or university transcripts must be submitted; hence, if you know the places where you are seeking to send transcripts, begin working on having them mailed to the appropriate places. Your original documents must be verified by an authorized person at the employment agency. Once this is done, have the documents copied so you can retain your original copies. It is definitely not advisable to submit your original documents because they can easily be misplaced and it may take you considerable time to replace them.

Interview Process

Once you have been shortlisted, you will have to go through an interview process. The interview gives you an opportunity to represent yourself face-to-face with your potential employer or their representative. Your journey through college should have prepared you for the interview process; but if not, there is plenty of information on the internet. You should also do some research regarding the institution from which you are seeking employment as this will assist you in the interview.

Upon completion of your interview, you will be informed as to when you can expect to hear back from the employer. If you are successful in getting the job, you will be given further instructions, and you will need to get yourself together mentally, physically, and emotionally. Make all the arrangement in terms of travel, accommodation, clothing, etc. that will prepare you for the first day on the job.

Chapter 4:

No Signature, No Employment

You signed on the dotted line. Hence the deal has been sealed, and now come the expectations. In your contract as a new teacher, you will have been hired to teach in a specific area or discipline. This may be as a general music teacher, an orchestra director, or a band or choir director. Generally, the contract will outline all the duties, roles, and responsibilities you are required to carry out in your new position. In addition to completing the contract, you should request to meet with the principal of the school, or the person they have delegated to represent them in this capacity, to go over the school's mission statement, goals, and objectives, and to clarify or discuss in more detail the school's expectation of you.

Contract

A contract is an agreement between the employer and the employee. You, as a newly hired teacher, should be familiar with all the details of the contract before signing it. This becomes a legally binding document once it is signed and dated by both parties. Make sure that you ask questions about any information in the document that is not clear. For example, under "job description," the last item is typically something like "…and any other duties as assigned by the employer or immediate supervisor." You would want to know what these other duties might entail.

Before signing a document, you can also seek advice from a professional, such as a lawyer or union representative. The contract should include your job description, hours of work, leave and vacation time, and your salary scale, as well as the terms and agreements around termination, resignation, and retirement.

Too often, people sign a contract without going through the details or understanding what they are signing—because they are caught up in the excitement of getting a new job. Then later when they decide to make a career change or retire, they may find out that they are not qualified or entitled to certain benefits. For example, in The Bahamas, teachers in the government system who reach their year of retirement may have to work additional time to compensate for the extra days they were given throughout the years, such as sick days or study leave.

Mission Statement, Goals, and Objectives

As a new teacher at a school, you will want to study the school's mission statement, goals, and objectives so that when planning and organizing your scheme of work units, forecast, and lesson plans, you will be in line with the school's goals and objectives. It will place you in a better position to gather support from administration and the school board if you can show them that you are designing or building a program that will contribute significantly to achieving the school's mission, goals, and objectives.

A school's mission statement outlines the reason school exists. Knowing the mission statement gives you a general overview of what the school is all about, and it sets the tone for everyone to follow, including parents, students, administration, faculty, and staff. Hence, whatever you plan to do as it relates to carrying out your job must be in line with the school's mission statement.

Goals are more specific in terms of outlining what the end results should be so as to accomplish the reason for the school's existence. Your goals must be aligned with the school's goals in order for there to be a win-win situation. If you accomplish your personal goals and they are not complementing the school's goals, then you are working in isolation. An analogy of this is a relay team. The goal of a relay team is to get the baton around the track before the other teams. If one person on a team runs his or her personal best, then drops the baton or makes a bad exchange because they decided to celebrate prematurely, then the entire team will suffer and not achieve the overall goal, even though one person would have broken his or her own record.

Another analogy—using music as it relates to accomplishing a personal goal and not the overall goal—would be a person playing a solo in a band performance and playing it so beautifully but at the wrong time—thus causing the entire band to sound chaotic and out of tune.

Objectives are the means by which you intend to achieve your goals. These are stated in behavioral terms and they outline the various steps that will be taken by the various stakeholders in order to achieve the overall goals of the school. I had the opportunity to speak with a new music teacher who had been teaching for less than three years, and she was ready to quit and move on to another career. She said that the last straw for her was when she took her students outside to engage them in an activity relating to her topic, and then received a negative report from the powers that be, stating that she was outside playing with her students. To me, this was either a clear case of misunderstanding between the parties or a sign that the powers that be were not current and not accepting of the strategies that new teachers are engaging in with their students in order to achieve their lesson objectives. Again, your personal objectives should be aligned with the school's objectives so that the entire team can reach their destination.

Meet the Principal

It is important to meet with the principal because they may have a vision and want the music department to contribute to it—despite, or in addition to, the school's mission statement, goals, and objectives. The principal is like a conductor, and he has to lead and direct all personnel on staff and keep them in harmony with each other. The music department may play a leading or supportive role in the life of the school, depending on the principal's directorship.

Meeting with the principal also places you in a better position to receive resources, as the entire school is competing for the typically limited amount of resources. Those staff who are in accord with the principal, and or who are consistent and persistent, tend to get their needs met more often and more quickly. As the old saying goes: the squeaky wheel gets the oil.

Self-Expectation

You should have your own expectations as to what your program will be like based on your prior knowledge and experience and on the position you were hired for. For example, if you were hired to build or maintain a concert band, you should know if you want to enter competitions, put on concerts and recitals, attend clinics, or invite guest conductors to work with your band—just to name a few possibilities. A balance must be struck between all the variables: the school's mission statement, goals, and objectives; the vision of the powers that be; and your personal expectations.

Your expectations may also be affected by other factors, such as the size of the school, the grade levels, the number of teachers in your department, and whether you are the Head of the Department or not.

Your school may have more than one music teacher and you may not be the Head of the Department. Therefore, your decision-making will be affected not only by the principal but also by the Head of Department.

Your school may be a very large school with a director of bands, and you may have been hired to direct one or more of the instrumental ensembles. Some of the more common ones are: concert bands, marching bands, jazz bands, orchestras, drum and bugle corps, recorder ensembles, brass quintets, and string quartets.

Your school may be a very small school, and the numbers coming to you for music may not be enough to maintain a marching band; and having a marching band may have been one of your expectations.

When I began teaching as a trained teacher, I was hired as a band teacher and I expected to hit the ground running. However, due to the lack of resources, I had to put plans in place to acquire the much-needed resources before realizing my expectations. One of those plans was to repair the instruments that were fixable and get them into circulation as soon as possible. Having an accommodating Head of Department made this process easy because she allowed me the time to work on the instruments. All of the above must be taken into consideration when planning your personal goals and objectives to achieve your expectations.

Chapter 5:

Know What You Have, Know What You Need

It is the most important event in the life of your school band, so you go to school one hour earlier to ensure that everything is in order before your students arrive. To your surprise, the band room door has already been opened, and when you step inside, all the instruments are gone except the damaged ones. What do you do? One must come to the realization that the expectation of the school, the principal, or the powers that be may not be practical because of the lack of resources. As the expert, it would be your responsibility to inform and educate the principal or the powers that be of what is needed in order to build the desired program. The first thing to be done before any work starts is to take an inventory of all available resources and facilities that would be at your disposal in order to teach, conduct rehearsals, and host meetings and special events.

Accountability is especially paramount if you are a band director or music teacher where tens of thousands of dollars are entrusted to you by way of expensive instruments and equipment. If you can show that you are a responsible, resourceful, and accountable person, this will work in your favor in future endeavors. A music department is probably the most or one of the most expensive departments to maintain. For this reason, it may be the first department from which funds are deducted when there is a need for school budget cuts.

Ironically, I built a band program that did many performances leading to the donation of instruments and to financial contributions for the school. The band for the most part was self-sufficient, and the funds the band brought in were sometimes used to finance other aspects of the school. Building a band to this level is highly beneficial because there will be no need to worry about budget cuts due to the fact that the band will be able to sustain itself.

From my experience, music teachers have typically not been doing a good job with their inventory and resources, although there are some who would be able to provide you with an accurate list of their instruments and resources at a moment's notice. The consistency in the way I organized my instruments on the shelf or in storage at the end of each day allowed me, at a quick glance, to tell whether an instrument was missing or not. You can only achieve this through an organized storage system. Hence, a thorough inventory and signing over of same should be carried out.

Conducting the Inventory

Request from the principal, or from the person who is responsible for the physical plant, an inventory of the instruments and equipment that are in storage. These records should also indicate if any instruments or equipment are out on loan, at the repair shop, or at some other storage location. This list is important in order for you to give an accurate account of everything in your inventory.

The inventory process should also be used to organize and label instruments according to their condition. State whether instruments are new, in good condition, in fair condition, or damaged. It is a good idea to use a color code when categorizing the instruments and equipment. This can be done by sticking colored stickies on the instrument case in an easily identifiable place, so you will be able to see the colors when the cases are stored on the shelves. In order to avoid mixing up instruments and cases, you can mark the instruments with the corresponding number on their case. This can be done with number stickers or by using a paint pen.

At one point in time, I had a serious problem with students taking instruments home without permission. To combat that problem, I wrote large numbers on the bell of the instruments with a white paint pen, and the students did not like this because they felt it ruined the appearance of the instrument. They would play the instruments in school, but they did not want to play them in public because everybody would know that the instrument did not belong to them. This also encouraged them to bring their personal instruments to school, thus reducing instrument shortage.

During the inventory process, one should have the serial number, make, and model of all the instruments and equipment recorded. This will be useful in the event of lost or stolen items and also with regard to rentals and signing out instruments to students. The instrument can be easily verified when and if the need arises. I, myself, benefitted from the recording of instrument serial numbers. On more than one occasion, I retrieved instruments from siblings of former band members who would have graduated and never returned their borrowed instrument. In each case, the students said that the instrument was given to them by their older sibling, not knowing that the instrument belonged to the school.

Another experience I had involving missing instruments was at the time of a summer break while repairs were being conducted. Two brand new Holton trumpets were stolen out of their cases in the cupboard of the band storage room. Although I never recovered those trumpets, I was able to give an accurate report to the police, referencing the description and serial numbers of the trumpets in the event they were found.

The takeaway you can learn from the above experience is that while work is being carried out in your music or band room, you should always be present or else have someone there to ensure that nothing is tampered with or goes missing. In the event that someone cannot be present, the instruments and equipment should be moved to another secured location until the work being done is completed.

In another incident, a colleague of mine, who is a music teacher at a small school, told me that the school was broken into and all of his wind instruments were stolen. The first thing I asked him was: Did he have the serial numbers of the instruments so the instruments could be easily identified, if found. He said no; he only knew the brand name of the instruments. Hence, this was a classic case of not taking a thorough inventory. Since then, the school has installed an alarm system and is in the process of purchasing some new instruments. I recommended that he record all the relevant information for the new instruments.

At another school where I worked, there was a break-in, and a sousaphone, a trombone, and a trumpet were stolen from the band room. The outside area of the band room was surrounded by iron gates and secured with pad locks. The entrance door to the room was also secured with a padlock. However, on the inside of the band room the cupboards were not secured with locks, and even if they had been secured, there was not enough space in the cupboards to secure instruments the size of a sousaphone. Therefore, take nothing for granted when securing your instruments and equipment.

Individuals can take advantage of any weakness in your security measures to steal an instrument, especially those who may come in contact with your environment on a daily or weekly basis and who know the security faults. During your inventory process, make note of the security measures currently in place and indicate if they need to be upgraded. An alarm system should always be a part of the security measures used to protect your instruments and equipment.

I would like to add here that the cheaper models of some equipment and instruments do not have a clear set of serial numbers. In this case, you can imprint, with a sharp object, either the serial numbers or an identifiable mark. Also, make sure you mark your instrument or equipment in an inconspicuous place so that only you would be able to identify it in the event it was stolen.

Just recently, a colleague of mine called me and said that his car had been broken into and his trumpet and car battery stolen. He wanted me to get the word out to fellow band directors to keep an eye out for persons who might try to sell the instrument or show up to their rehearsal with the instrument. I asked him for the serial number of the instrument, but he didn't know. The description he gave was that it was a silver King trumpet with a visible soldered brace on the lead pipe and ML marked on the end of the bell and the middle of the second valve. In this case, at least he was able to give an identifiable marking that could assist with retrieving his instrument.

Inventory should also include furniture. You have to make sure that there is sufficient furniture and the right type of furniture to accommodate the students that are coming to you for lessons. Special areas like a music room or science lab require furniture that is not used in regular classrooms.

In the school where I taught, my band room was small, and it was also used to teach music theory and history. Therefore, the room had to be transformed from a theory setting to a practical setting on a daily basis. During the theory classes, students used the folding desk that had to be moved to the side in order to set up chairs for the band class. It is not appropriate for band members to sit in chairs with desk tops attached to them because this is not conducive to holding an instrument correctly and maintaining correct posture. The folding desks were better because, when moved to the side, they required less space than the regular stand-alone student desk.

In order to create extra space for the students and to allow them to be comfortable, I gave up my teacher's desk space by putting the desk against the wall. I decided that it was more important for me to be able to accommodate additional students than to be able to sit behind a teacher's desk.

An ideal situation for you to function efficiently, in a classroom that has to be transformed because of a space problem, is to have desks where the top can be folded down and out of the way of the instrument, thus saving a lot of time. This was not the case for me, however; I had to make the best of the furniture that was provided.

Like the instruments, your band room chairs should also be marked in a way that is easily identifiable, especially when the chairs have to be used elsewhere. During assemblies, my band students brought the band room chairs to the verandah. At the end of the performances, I would debrief the students and tell them to secure their chairs in the band room. Then when they were all gone, it amazed me that I would still see a couple of chairs left on the verandah.

As a result of the clear marking on the chairs, they were not usually taken by other persons. If they were taken, then I would be able to search the school campus and locate them due to the marking.

Completion of Inventory

Once the inventory process has been completed, you will know if you have all the resources to accomplish the mission, goals, and objectives discussed in the previous chapter. In a perfect world, you will have all the resources you need and more. However, this is usually not the case. In all my years of teaching, I have never heard a music teacher say that they had all of the instruments and equipment needed to effectively run their program the way they had envisioned.

There is one instance where I can remember having more than enough Standard of Excellence band method books. Somehow the requisition list for books that I had provided to the school board was mistakenly ordered twice. This was due to a breakdown in communication somewhere along the line.

If your inventory comes up short upon completion, you will have to decide what to do to make the situation work. Here are three things that can be done in order to get immediate results.

First, you must inform the principal or powers-that-be of your findings once you have completed your inventory. Provide a list of instruments and equipment that are needed, along with price quotes, and see if there is a budget for new instruments and equipment. Some institutions may require at least three quotes from reputable businesses. If there is a budget, inquire as to how they will go about purchasing the required items and the timeline in which the instruments should be delivered to the school.

I found that picking up the instruments or equipment was a quicker process for me once the check was provided because of my close proximity to the music stores. Also, it meant I could examine the instruments before they left the store. Sometimes adjustments had to be made to the order due to the store not having the correct amount of inventory or a better product may have come in since the quote was provided.

Second, this may be a school in which students are required or encouraged to purchase their personal instruments as a prerequisite for joining the music program. In this case, you will be able to carry on with your program without missing a beat.

Third, if you or the school have a good relationship with the surrounding schools or community bands, you may be able to borrow instruments, or to organize an exchange program where you can trade instruments you do not need or have an abundance of, with a school or community band that needs those instruments and may have the instruments that you need.

In my experience, some schools had special instruments that were not being used, such as bassoons, oboes, and French horns. This was due to the fact that students did not want to play these instruments because they were not popular and they had not been exposed to them. In other cases, teachers were not comfortable or familiar with teaching these instruments so they did not introduce them to their students. Therefore, if you would like to gain access to these instruments, check to see if they might be available.

Fundraisers

There are other ways one can acquire the much-needed instruments and equipment, and thus have their program up and running in a timely manner. However, these require more time and a little more creativity. Here are a few ideas to consider…

First, establish a committee to organize fundraisers with the goal of generating monies to purchase instruments and equipment. The number of fundraisers can vary based on your budget and the committee's creativity.

Second, send letters out to the business locations in the areas surrounding your school, seeking sponsorship to purchase instruments and equipment. In return, you may be in the position to offer a musical performance for a special event the business may be putting on, such as a Christmas party, a product promotion the business may be launching, or a special program.

Third, you can organize a Fun Run/Walk ending with a health fair where participants have to pay a registration fee, thus generating funds to purchase instruments and equipment.

Fourth, you can tap into the alumni association of the school and request that they donate or raise funds through their association to purchase instruments and equipment. Some of these individuals will have businesses of their own and may be able to assist and to use their influence in their circle to contribute to the music department.

Fifth, you can host a talent show at the school, charging students and their families and the wider community a small fee to view the various talents on display, such as singing, dancing, instrumental solos, magic acts, and juggling, just to name a few.

Sixth, you can have a cookie drive where each student is given a case of assorted cookies to sell and a prize can be given to the student who sells the most cookies.

Seventh, you can organize a raffle draw, where individuals and businesses can donate tangible items to be given as prizes, such as a car, a cruise, a holiday round trip ticket for two, household appliances, and more. Have students and staff sell raffle books to their friends and families and throughout their community.

Take some time to decide what kind of fundraisers you would like to get started on, and then proceed with the planning, organizing, and executing.

In the meantime, you must begin with what you have and alter your ensembles to accommodate the instrumentation available. For example, you may be hired to teach a marching band but may be lacking percussion instruments. Therefore, build a concert band while waiting to obtain the required marching percussions. In the meantime, you can still take the band members on the field to learn basic marching fundamentals.

My first formal teaching job was taking on the role of a band teacher in a senior high school, grades 10 through 12. There were only a few instruments and the school had only a concert band that did not perform outside of the classroom very often. Based on my background, experience, and expectations, I set out to improve the situation. Long story short, I used my relationship with another band director and a band I played in to borrow a few marching percussions, and within a very short time the school band was outside marching.

I also used this as a means of getting support from the powers that be to purchase the much-needed instruments for the band. Everyone was excited to hear the band marching on the school's campus. The band became the talk of the school because they were sounding great and this was the first time ever that the school had a marching band. What I did was make the band relevant, and the powers that be wanted the band to play for a number of engagements. This is when I told them that the band could not perform for the engagements because the students were using borrowed instruments that had to be returned. Upon hearing this, it reinforced in their minds that the music department was lacking instruments and equipment. After this, buying instruments was a matter of urgency for the music department.

In a similar occurrence, one of my colleagues built his band program by using a lot of his personal instruments, and even had to pay to get some of the school instruments repaired because those in charge continued to make promises without delivering. His band had a number of engagements and special requests to play for events, but the powers that be had not made good on their promise to assist with the purchasing and repair of instruments. My colleague said that were it not for the students, he would have pulled his instruments out of the school system.

Sometimes the powers that be really do not understand what it takes to develop and maintain a music program. Therefore, the band director or music teacher must sell the music program by making persons aware of the various ensembles and possibilities, and highlighting the positives that can come about as a result of a vibrant music program in the school. This can only come about, however, if the department is furnished with the much-needed inventory.

Chapter 6:

Inferior Instruments, Inferior Sound

In a perfect world, instruments and equipment should be of good quality, and also uniform as far as possible for a number of reasons—including sound, looks, and life span.

Quality Sound

Two different bands can play the same band arrangement and sound totally different. This can be as a result of many variables, and the quality of the instruments and equipment is a critical factor. The number one goal of having an instrument is to play it. The number one goal for playing that instrument is to produce a sound. Therefore, you want to hear a good quality sound coming from that instrument, and this can only be the case if the instrument is of good quality. Hence, you want an instrument that is of the best quality and able to produce the best sound.

Instruments of the same make and model tend to be consistent with tuning and blend better when played together. This is very important for your band because the band is made up of individuals who play together in a section, such as a trumpet or a clarinet section, and the various sections form the band. Instruments of the same make and model generally have the same intonation, and this relates to how various notes are in tone with each other.

In contrast, inferior instruments may be extremely difficult to play in tone, as the intonation from one note to the next may be totally off. In the hands of a professional, it may be possible to manipulate the instrument and get it to sound halfway decent, but a beginner student may find it difficult to play it in tone. It is not advisable for a beginner to learn on an instrument that is not in tone with itself, because the beginner may develop a wrong sense of pitch, as they will tend to rely on holding a fingering or position and play whatever note comes out with that particular fingering or position. Consequently, when they are given a quality instrument, they will play it out of tone and not be aware that they are doing so. I experience this quite often when a student is playing an instrument where a key is not closing properly and they are holding the correct fingering but a different pitch is coming out. The student will typically say that they are playing the right note because they cannot differentiate one pitch from the other.

Uniformity

Your band should not only sound good, it should also look good. "Uniform" not only refers to the type of clothes your band is wearing, it also refers to the way your band is marching—the formations, the lines, the spaces, the way the instruments are held and carried, as well as the color and make of the instruments. If it's possible, all the instruments should be the same color—for example, brass, silver, or some other color that complements your school's band uniform. Encourage parents who are buying instruments for their children—and also sponsors purchasing instruments for your school—to buy instruments that match the color scheme you are working with.

A uniformed band will enhance the overall presentation of your band during performances, and it will give band members a sense of belonging and a sense of pride to be part of a prestigious organization. Uniformity is an important element as it is one of the major categories on a score sheet for band competitions. An analogy can be made with military personnel. If you dress a soldier in camouflage clothing designed for combat, and give him or her the necessary equipment, he or she will feel indispensable. Psychologically speaking, being uniformed adds to the overall sound of your band. Hence, looks may be associated with sound.

Good Quality

Instruments of good quality tend to have a longer life span and require less repair—due to the superior materials and craftmanship. In most cases, your school band instruments are played, on a daily basis, by multiple students coming to band class from the various grade levels. This naturally means a lot of wear and tear on the instruments, and even more so with students who are not holding the instrument correctly and/or are not handling the instrument with care. Under such conditions, good quality instruments will hold up much longer.

In contrast, instruments that are poorly made tend to fall apart sooner, thus requiring more repairs. We often make a joke about the poor-quality instruments typically made in China—that if you look at them too hard, they will fall apart. Looking at it from another angle, however, it may be in the best interest of parents to purchase a student model instrument for their child because some children are not 100 percent sure of the instrument they want to play. They may decide after a couple of weeks that they want to play a different instrument or do not want to play at all. Then, the parent is left to sell the instrument or give it away. Not until the child shows interest in sticking with the instrument for the long haul should the parent consider upgrading to a more professional instrument. With this in mind, it is important that the child takes care of their student model instrument in order for it to last until a better one is purchased.

Due to the lack of funding, your school instruments are typically not serviced and repaired in a timely manner—thus adding to the deterioration process of the instruments. The instruments that are of poorer quality are made of materials that are softer, and the keys and body of the instrument bend more easily than those of better-quality instruments. As mentioned earlier, holding these instruments and setting them down incorrectly, or pressing the keys too hard while playing, can bend the keys.

However, if the school is not in a position to provide its own funding, then you will have to work with the instruments and equipment that may have been acquired from various sources. Having some instruments is better than having none. You can always upgrade as your program develops, gets popular, and gains exposure.

Chapter 7:

No Students, No Band

Recruiting students for your music program is probably the most important step in achieving the mission, goals, and objectives of your school. If there were no students, there would be no need for teachers, and consequently, if there were no music students, there would be no need for a band program. Hence, your job depends on your student population. There are a number of ways to recruit students for your music program and some of them will be discussed in this chapter.

Existing Band Members

Depending on your new position, you may be replacing a band director at a school with an established music program, or you may be hired by a school to build an entirely new program. In the case of the former, your task will be easier because you will be coming into a school with students who are already band members and who are familiar with the school's culture and operating system as far as the music program is concerned.

It would be a good idea, if possible, to meet with the outgoing band director and have him or her introduce you to the current band members. This can take the form of a social event, be it formal or informal. Such an event will serve three main goals. First, to say thank you to the outgoing band director for the work he or she has accomplished thus far. Second, to introduce and welcome the incoming band director for accepting the challenge to continue building on the band's success and take the band to new heights. Third, to serve as an ice breaker—to meet the band students and interact with them to find out what their aspirations are in relation to the band. This kind of event will allow for a smooth transition, and you can get a heads up on how to move forward with your strategizing.

Meeting face-to-face with the outgoing band director would be ideal, but this may not always be possible. However, you can try to connect by other means of communication—via telephone or on one of the many social media platforms. The idea is to find out all the do's and don'ts that made the program successful or non-successful; to find out about projects in the pipeline, whether big or small, that will affect the music program; and to find out about persons in the community or corporate world who have partnered with the school and with whom you will want to maintain a mutual relationship in the future.

The former band director will also be able to fill you in on the strengths and weaknesses of the existing band students. Knowing who are the leaders and the go-getters will be to your advantage. You can use these band members to help recruit students to be a part of your program. Students tend to have a greater influence over their peers than adults do, especially as it relates to various extracurricular activities.

On the flip side of things, you will want to be aware of students who are comfortable with the status quo. No two persons are alike, and therefore your teaching style and the way you structure your practice may be different from the style and structure of the former band director. Some students may take a while to adapt, and you might hear them say that their former band teacher did it this way or that way…. Your job is to make them aware that you are a different person and also to be consistent in the way you execute your daily routine. You may still lose one or two students but the remainder will fall in line with your program.

I had new students who had played an instrument already with other band directors, and then they came to join the school band and they wanted to dictate to me what part they wanted to play, based on what they had played in their other band, or what part they preferred to play. I told them that it didn't work like that and that they had to play the part that was assigned to them. As a result of this, I lost a few band members. Some students believe that they are less of a player if you assign them to play a second or third part. They do not understand that you are looking for an overall blend and balance for the band.

In order to achieve such a balance, you may have to assign your strongest player to play a second or third part instead of the first part, depending on the music arrangement. In some arrangements, the second part may have the melody or be more challenging than the first. A good strategy is to allow your strongest sight reader to learn multiple parts because then they will be able to move from one part to the next at a moment's notice. For example, you may have two persons playing first trumpet and the second trumpet player is missing. The trumpet player you had learning both parts would then be able to move to the second trumpet part, hence covering all the parts.

Parent Meeting

The first Parent Teacher Association meeting for the school year would be another great time and place to recruit students for your band or music program. This is the time when you will see the majority of your student population's parents. At subsequent meetings, parent attendance is usually smaller than at the initial meeting. The next time you will likely see a lot of parents will be at report card collection day, and even then, not all parents will show up.

For the first meeting, you can get permission to set up an information booth where you will be able to advertise your music or band program, both before and after the meeting. While parents are coming in, they can receive relevant information about the music program via brochures and flyers explaining what the program is all about and how it can benefit their child or children. You can have instruments on display and even have existing band members in their band uniform assisting with advertising and/or performing on some of the instruments. Ensure also that information is available on where parents can purchase instruments and/or accessories for their child or children.

A video presentation of the band would also be a good idea to show at this time. The video can highlight the band performing at various events, students speaking about their experiences as part of the band, and students engaged in rehearsal and instructional periods.

At the end of the Parent Teacher Association meeting, you can have parents with their children try out the various instruments to see which one they would be most interested in and what would be most suitable for their physique. For this process, ensure that the necessary disinfecting and sanitizing products are in place, such as sterisol germicide, wipes, hand sanitizer, hand towel, garbage bin, and replacement bags. Also, have additional mouthpieces, straps, and reeds for the woodwind instruments. As for the percussion sections, because of the loud nature of the instruments, the players will have to try out on drum pads or meet in a separate room.

Parents will be more at ease if they can see that you have a safe, clean, and healthy environment, as well as an organized and efficient operation. One's first impression is a big deal, and a great impression will translate into new members joining your music or band program.

Recruiting Non-Music Majors

The majority of the band members will come from the students who are enrolled in the music program and who are taking band or instrumental ensemble classes. However, I find it to be the case that typically many other students enrolled in the school can play a musical instrument. Some of them are not aware that they can become a member of the school band or music ensemble; and some of them would like to become members of the band but have conflicting schedules based on their program and the time of band rehearsals. Others may play an instrument that is not taught in the music program; for example, a student may play the violin but the school has a concert band and not an orchestra. And others may feel that the school band is not appealing to them based on its repertoire or that the band is simply not at their level.

A recruitment strategy to attract students who are unaware of the fact that they could join the school's band, if they wanted to, is to send out an advertisement via the school's social media platforms. Announcements can also be made regularly via the school's Public Announcement System, and you can place flyers around the school's campus, especially at the beginning of a new school year. This tends to be the time when most of the clubs are advertising, promoting, and competing for members.

When I first started teaching at the high school, the girls' basketball coach used to put up his recruitment signs even before the new school year started. In addition, he had rehearsals every day, which explains why his team was the number one high school girls' basketball team in The Bahamas for many years. I took a page from the coach's book as it related to recruiting new students and to having practice on a consistent and daily basis. It is also beneficial to know the meeting times for the various clubs so you can schedule your band rehearsal times to accommodate students who wish to be in the band and in other clubs.

Another Physical Education teacher, who coached Track and Field, visited the music room and was surprised to see that so many of his athletes were members of the school band. This opened his eyes to the many talents of these students and to the fact that we had to work together more closely for the betterment of the students.

When I taught in the senior high school, most of the clubs met in the afternoon, especially the sporting clubs during their scheduled season. About 50 percent of my band members were athletes or were part of a cadet program that met in the afternoons. For this reason, I held band rehearsals on Monday, Wednesday, and Friday mornings at 8:00 a.m. for one hour and then also during lunch times to accommodate students that were not enrolled in the band classes.

In the case of students who play an instrument that is not offered within the music program, be creative and find a way to include them in the band. For example, you can create a mixed ensemble and have them perform as a separate group. Also, they can play a solo piece on their instrument and be accompanied by the band. When the band is playing an arrangement that does not call for their instrument, they can play a percussion instrument that may be needed or perhaps learn to play another instrument. A student who plays a string instrument from the violin family may find it fairly easy to learn a bass or lead guitar that they can play with your concert band.

Most band arrangements have the music for these instruments, and these are the instruments that are usually lacking in your school band. A student who plays the piano may find it easy to learn a melodic percussion instrument, such as a glockenspiel, marimba, or xylophone because the keys are arranged similarly to the keys of the piano. If these instruments are not available, then it would be even easier for the student to play the percussion part on a keyboard by adjusting the settings to the desired percussion instrument sound.

In the case of students who are not interested because of the repertoire, try to include a variety of genres in your repertoire so that students will be more interested in joining the band. For example, there may be a student who is only interested in playing jazz music but the school does not have a jazz band. By adding a few jazz selections in your concert or marching band's repertoire, and inviting the student to take some of the solos, he or she may be more inclined to join the band.

Students who feel that they are above the level of the band can be placed in an ensemble with the more advanced players; for example, a woodwind trio, a string quartet, or a brass quintet. This grouping can play at special events, such as concerts, competitions, recitals, and festivals. You can also ask an advanced student to lead a particular section of the band so they can assist in teaching the weaker students. Peer teaching will give them something to look forward to and motivate them to becoming an integral part of the band.

Over time, I came across a number of students who played an instrument but did not play in their school's band. Once I know that a student plays an instrument, I always ask them which school they attend and if they play in the school band. Some of them reply that it doesn't make sense for them to join their school band because they are above the level of the band. In that case, I encourage them to find some way to assist their school's band. I also try to reach out to the music teacher or band director and make sure they are informed of the talent they have at their school.

Making the band more attractive can also assist with recruitment. For example, you can ask band members to wear a band jacket or t-shirt on a particular day of the week or to wear some kind of badge or pin identifying them as band members or as part of the music program.

Lastly, one of the most effective ways to recruit new band students is by word of mouth, and what better way than to have band members recruited by their peers. In most cases, students are influenced by their peers, and their peers will be able to motivate them and sell the benefits of joining the band program.

Chapter 8:

To Plan Is To Succeed

Protocol must be established before conducting an actual rehearsal. These procedures will make your life in the school environment a lot easier and more enjoyable. As mentioned in the previous chapter, your scheduled rehearsal time and location outside of regular band class time should be clearly outlined and made known to all persons concerned.

Seek Approval

You must be mindful that you are teaching in a school where there are many people involved and all must work together for one common goal. Everyone believes that their work is just as important or more important than yours. Before scheduling your days, times, and locations of rehearsal, you will want to first seek approval from the principal, who will typically be in charge of the overall scheduling for the entire school. Once approval has been granted, you can move on to the next step, which is to make your schedule known to the various persons involved.

The principal, or the administrator in charge of substitution, will have to be aware of your practice days and times because they will have to know when and if they can use you as a substitute in the event a teacher is away.

Also, teachers will need a copy of your approved schedule because they too have events, meetings, and activities going on where they may need to use a particular room or space. If they have your schedule on hand, then there won't be a problem with double booking. Too often I have seen scheduling conflicts where two teachers are planning to use the same room or space at the same time. Typically, this is just a lack of communication or misinterpretation between the two parties.

Teachers may also need to know the level of sound that may be coming from your practice room or rooms in the event that they may have to use a room in close vicinity to yours for an activity that requires silence. Another reason that teachers might need to have your schedule is because they may need to use some of the students who are members of your band for certain activities.

As for your band students, they will need to know your schedule more so than any other stakeholder because it is all about them. They will need to include their rehearsal times on their daily timetables so they can manage their time effectively. Knowing the schedule will allow them to prepare for the particular rehearsal, whether it be concert band or marching band, and knowing the location will assist them in getting to the rehearsal in a timely manner. When I taught band in the high school, my morning rehearsals began at 8:00 a.m. Students used all sorts of excuses as to why they were late, and not knowing the rehearsal time was one of them. Often times I would see them hanging around outside the band room socializing with friends or eating breakfast, and then they would come to the rehearsal when they were good and ready. Granted, some of the excuses were no fault of the students because they were brought to school by parents who had no regard for the time.

I had a late policy, namely that the band room door would be closed at a particular time and not open until the completion of practice. In this case, some of the innocent suffered for the guilty but the punctuality improved. Some of the students who were brought to school by their parents encouraged their parents to bring them to school a little earlier. Also, more work got done during the rehearsal because it was void of the constant interruption of late arrivals.

Support staff such as the janitors or janitresses will also need to know your schedule due to the fact that they will be the person or persons responsible for cleaning the rooms and spaces in preparation for rehearsals.

School security will also need a copy of your schedule, so they will be more informed regarding the activities of the school in terms of the safety aspect. They will then know what to expect when they are making their rounds and routine checks of the buildings, yard, and spaces being occupied. I am often questioned by security as to what is happening on the school's campus during a particular day because they are not always informed by teachers of their extracurricular activities related to school.

I have experience on a number of occasions where special guests were treated in a hostile manner by security because security was not formally updated as to visitors who were invited on campus by the teachers. On the other hand, in some cases, security members were lacking in the ability to use their discretion, given that guests were known to them, having visited the campus many times before.

Keep Good Records

Along with your rehearsal schedule, ensure that all teachers receive a list of all students in the band. This is of utmost importance, especially if the teacher teaches one or more of the students on the list or has them as a member of their homeroom class. By checking the schedule, the teacher will know the whereabouts of their students in the event they are late or absent from the registration period as a result of band rehearsal or performance.

During my rehearsals in the mornings, I kept a register of the students attending band rehearsals so the teachers were able to cross-reference and use it as a check and balance to maintain a more accurate register, whether it be homeroom or subject teachers. This was also important to weed out the students who used being at band practice as an excuse for skipping registration or a particular class.

I also kept a register of all the students attending performances to be used for future references such as rewards and awards, and also to determine who were delinquent band members. I had a policy that if students missed too many performances, they would be suspended from the band for a certain length of time.

Ensuring that teachers have a list of all the band members also assists in the discipline aspect of the band. Teachers can inform the band director of students who may require disciplinary actions. Some students behave differently when they are in the presence of teachers other than their homeroom teacher, especially if they feel that the teacher does not know them or their name.

Have a Good Working Relationship with Colleagues

No matter what, when there are two or more people in the same environment, there will be conflicts and disagreements. Your goal is to strive to develop a good working relationship with all of your colleagues. This means that you should agree to disagree. Seek to have a mutual relationship in which everyone wins. This can only be achieved through communicating and conducting yourself in a professional manner. Treat each other with respect and show concern for one another.

Every school is set up differently, and you may be in an environment where the classrooms are closely connected. Hence, because of the sound level, it is not conducive for a music room to be next to, or in close proximity to, other classrooms. In the high school where I taught, my classroom was adjacent to an art room and separated by just a sheetrock partition. If I hadn't established a good working relationship with the art teachers, the situation could have gotten ugly on numerous occasions.

Some days the teacher would tell me that her students were enjoying the music the band was playing while they were working on their drawing, painting, or sculpture. Other days, I would hear banging on the partition and someone saying, "Keep it down, we are trying to concentrate over here."

To make matters worse, sometimes the band would be working on an arrangement to play for a performance the following day. Other times, the teacher would come over and request that the band not play because her students were being graded by external examiners for their national exam. However, as a result of communication and mutual respect, we were able to work something out every time.

In the same school, as a result of space issues, during section practice I had to send a section or two to the outside veranda, and this sometimes proposed a problem. The students were in close proximity to another art classroom window, and what made matters worse was that the teacher's desk was positioned by the window. Therefore, when it became unbearable, the teacher would come to me and say that the students were disturbing her. In addition to the sound of the instruments, the teacher sometimes remarked on the inappropriate language and conversation coming from the students. Therefore, when students had to utilize the veranda, I would try to send the quieter instruments, such as the woodwind section, and I would ask the students to pay attention to their vocabulary.

In a perfect world, the music department should have a separate block away from the other classrooms so other classes will not be disturbed, and so there is no interruption regarding the flow of your rehearsal or your instructional class time. If this is not the case, then you must seek to get your music room soundproofed, thus allowing your band to play at any time and at all dynamic levels.

As you can see from the above, you have to be creative and be able to adjust at a moment's notice as a result of the spacing and layout of your school. Having a good working relationship with your colleagues will make your experience a much more productive and enjoyable one.

Chapter 9:
Great Rehearsals, Great Performances

Your architect draws you a plan for a square building 20' x 20' x 20' x 20' and you give the plan to your contractor, who then lays out a foundation 20' x 20' x 20' x 18'. What would be the result when your building was constructed? Most certainly it would not be a square, and the result of not following the plan would cause everything related to the building to be off. And fixing the problem would cost a considerable amount of unbudgeted funds and time.

In the same way, when teaching students, the foundation is of utmost importance if they are to excel in their endeavors. Students should always be encouraged to maintain best practices because developing bad habits will always hinder their ability to get to the next level.

The rehearsal or band classes should be conducted in an organized, consistent, and exciting way, thus accommodating all students in order to achieve your lesson plan's objectives for the day. You should strive to ensure that all your students develop a strong foundation and leave with a sense of achievement.

Be Prepared

Valuable time is wasted when you are not prepared. In order to be an effective teacher and one who maximizes time, you need to be organized. In order to be organized, you must prepare well in advance before the class. In addition to your forecast and lesson plan, the classroom must be a safe, clean, well-lit, and ventilated environment. The furniture should be arranged in order to enhance the lesson and make your classroom an inviting and comfortable environment for your students. Also, the method books, sheet music, instrument accessories, and music stands should be in place. If you are using technology, such as a projector, promethean board, laptop, or computer, test them before the class begins.

I have observed teachers (whom I supervised during their annual assessment) using technology as a resource and taking a considerable amount of time away from their lesson because they were not prepared and proactive. One teacher even left his class unattended to look for accessories for his laptop—which is totally unacceptable. In other cases, teachers were unable to use the technology because of problems connecting to the internet. Make sure you have practiced with the technology you plan to use, and always have a plan B—because technology can malfunction. In any event, technology should be used to complement or enhance your lesson; it should not be the main teacher.

If you are using a dry erase or chalk board for note taking, demonstrating or mounting resource material, put the relevant information on the board before the class time. Also, ensure that you have additional markers in the event that your marker dries out during your instruction period. On a number of occasions, I have had students sent to me for dry erase markers because their teacher's marker had dried out during their lesson. This takes time away from formal instruction and places your students at a disadvantage. And it can easily be avoided if you are prepared.

Being prepared also means anticipating student shortfalls. Some of them will come to class without their materials, such as pencils, erasers, notebooks, mouthpieces, reeds, straps, and even their instruments. Having an extra one or two of the various accessories will alleviate the loss of instructional time. In addition, you can seek permission to sell these items to students, thus making them accountable for their supplies, while also raising funds for your department.

Oftentimes, students come with their instrument not working properly, or it may malfunction during the class. Having a replacement instrument would be ideal in order not to waste instructional time on having to troubleshoot and repair the instrument. If you do not have a replacement instrument and the problem looks to be a quick fix—such as a spring that has come out of place or an unaligned valve—you can fix it or else point out the problem to the student so they can fix it. The more that students learn to troubleshoot and to carry out minor adjustments to their instrument, the less time you will have to take away from your instructional time.

Sometimes a student may say that their instrument is not playing or that a note is not coming out. Have them pass their instrument to another student, preferably a more advanced student, and ask that student to play the instrument. If there is a problem, the other student may know how to fix it, and if there is not a problem, then the first student may be doing something wrong.

It is important for new band directors or music teachers to put their foot down on day one, go over the classroom rules, address all discipline problems quickly, and be consistent. Addressing problems quickly and being consistent equals good classroom management skills. If you are consistent, students will learn what is expected of them and do what is required of them without having to be told. I have found from experience that students appreciate structure and a disciplined environment in spite of them being rebellious at times.

On a number of occasions, I have experienced the result of having a well-structured system in place for my students. My school band normally played for the school's weekly general assembly, and if for some reason I was not there, you would not have known it because the students would organize themselves, set up the band, and play for the assembly. This was also the case for the regular band class. In the event I was unable to start the class due to circumstances beyond my control, such as a visitor showing up at the door, the students would begin the class without me; and I would at times catch them imitating me teaching the class or conducting the band.

Teaching Your Lesson

All new teachers should have a prepared and up-to-date forecast and lesson plan to guide them during teaching their lesson or rehearsing their band. I will outline a 10-step general guideline that you can follow when conducting your rehearsal or teaching your class. Be mindful that these can be altered based on the type of ensemble, the class size, the availability of instruments, and the grade and skill level of the students.

First, at the beginning of your rehearsal, stand at the door and receive your students. Also, taking the register at this time can cut down on the loss of instructional time. Instruct students who bring their personal instrument to take their seats and assemble their instruments quietly. Tell students who are using the school's instruments to retrieve their assigned instrument, take their seats, and assemble their instruments quietly. All students must wait for the teacher's next instructions. In the event of a music theory class, tell students to take out their manuscript or workbook, head up their book with the standard information, and/or take notes that you have previously written on the board.

Second, once students assemble their instruments and are seated quietly waiting on the next set of instructions, you can guide them through the class or rehearsal, beginning with your introduction. Your introduction should be one that is relevant, stimulating, and that links or transitions the last topic to the new topic. Make students aware of the class objectives, which can be written on the board or projected from your device of choice. At this point, as a discipline measure for students who play their instrument out of turn, I may instruct them to put their instrument away so they will not be able to play for the rest of the class.

If there is a shortage of instruments, I also use this as a discipline strategy and a way to keep students focused at all times. The first student that makes a mistake as a result of not paying attention, or playing out of turn, must give their instrument to the student without an instrument. This keeps the students focused, and the student without an instrument watches with a keen eye to see who will be the next victim. Students love to play their instruments, so this strategy tends to keep them focused and not playing out of turn. If their instrument is taken away, they have to follow along and clap the rhythms that the class is playing.

Another strategy is to tell the student to stand for a specific time period or for the remainder of the class, while the other students are sitting down.

Third, guide them through the warm-up process. Begin with a breathing exercise that teaches students to breathe properly while playing their instrument. Breathing is the most important aspect of playing a wind instrument, because without air, there can be no sound. The combination of air and the various mouthpieces and reeds produces the vibration that oscillates air through the body of the instrument, thus making the instrument play. Ensure that students maintain correct posture during this exercise and throughout the entire class.

Students should sit forward in their chair, with back straight, feet flat on the ground, shoulders relaxed, and with the instrument held correctly in the rest position. Tell students to breathe in slowly through their nose until their lungs are filled, and then breathe out slowly through their mouth, thus emptying their lungs. A constant air flow should be maintained during this time. While breathing in, the chest should rise, and the abdomen moves outward as the lungs are filled; and while breathing out, the opposite occurs. If the shoulders are moving up and down during this exercise, they are doing it wrong.

After the breathing exercise, tell students to buzz in just their mouthpiece, as a means to loosen, warm up, and relax their lips. Let them practice the same breathing exercise while buzzing through their mouthpiece. Various pitches and rhythm exercises can also be played on the mouthpieces alone.

Fourth, instruct students to assemble their mouthpieces on their instruments in preparation for playing long notes. They can then play long notes up and down a given scale or with just one or two notes based on their skill level. In a beginners' class, tell students to play whatever note they can play during this exercise. Some brass players may be able to play low notes, while others may be able to play high notes. Playing long notes helps to strengthen a student's embouchure, which includes all the muscles involved in manipulating a sound from the instrument. A strong embouchure builds their endurance and improves their overall sound.

Fifth, use a band method book at the appropriate level for the class to work on various technical exercises that are part of your objectives for the lesson—such as slurs, staccatos, accents, dynamics, or various rhythm studies. In addition, you can write or project on the appropriate board your own exercises that you wish students to play.

Sixth, guide them through one or two sight reading exercises to develop their music reading skills. Sight reading is one of the greatest assets an instrumentalist can have, and the only way to develop this skill is through constant practice. During sight reading exercises, students should first look through their music in order to identify key signatures, time signatures, tempo, specific rhythms, accidentals, and performance directions. Students should then play through the music from beginning to end at a tempo in which they can play it with minimum mistakes. At the end of the play-through, you can point out to the students the areas of concern.

Seventh, direct students to work on a few bars or a section of a new piece of music that the band is learning for its repertoire. Students should spend the majority of time practicing what they do not know. This saves class or rehearsal time tremendously and allows the class to avoid playing the same section of music repeatedly and thus neglecting the other sections. A good strategy I learned in college to ensure that all the music is rehearsed is to start rehearsing the music a couple of bars from the end and then work backwards, instead of starting every rehearsal from the beginning.

Eighth, it is essential for students to leave with a sense of achievement; therefore, have them play a piece from the band's repertoire that they love to play or recap an exercise they would have played earlier from the method books. In the case of beginners, allow them to play the new note or notes they will have learned during the class.

Ninth, give students their homework, and then end the lesson by instructing students to return all borrowed music accessories, to clean their instruments of condensation, and to wipe off all fingerprints before securing them safely in their case.

Tenth, once all the instruments and equipment are accounted for and secured in the appropriate place, remind students of the next band practice and dismiss them in an orderly fashion.

As mentioned earlier, these are general guidelines to follow and you can adjust them based on your classroom set-up and the students in your class. During the class, you can add excitement in a number of ways. You can include rhythm games during the warm-up period. You can give students ear training by playing a note or a short melody and having them imitate what you play on their instrument. As a competition, you can have students play technical exercises by sections and at various speed levels. You can give a prize to the section that plays the fastest and with accuracy. Also, you can have a competition for who can hold a note the longest, thus building endurance.

From my experience, the above suggestions always bring joy and excitement to the class, as students love to compete. You as the teacher should demonstrate holding a note for a long period to show students that it can be done, as well as to motivate them to try to do the same.

Ensure that all the students are catered to during the instructional period because not all of them will be on the same level. Every class or band has students with different levels of ability; hence, while giving instructions, you must regularly assess if everyone is mastering the skills and concepts. A student that is lagging behind may have to be separated from the other students in order to work on playing a particular note or rhythm correctly before rejoining the class. In this way, you can keep all the students engaged, as opposed to them waiting while you are focusing on one student.

When you are working with a student or with a group of instruments on a particular section of the music, instruct the other students to focus on their music and follow along so they will not be lost when you are ready for them to play. Sometimes the students who are following may have the same rhythm as the students you are working with; hence, in following their music, they may also be able to correct music they were playing incorrectly.

Chapter 10:
Perfect Practice, Perfect Results

An important goal for you as band director should be to improve the standard of your band on a daily basis. This can only be done if the individual band members improve themselves daily. As the cliché goes, a chain is only as strong as its weakest link; hence, a band is only as strong as its weakest member. Imagine that you have a school band with all intermediate to advanced players and one elementary player, and your goal is to play a piece of music that the entire band can play correctly. As a result, your band would only be able to play elementary music.

For every hour of formal class time, students should spend at least two hours reinforcing the new concepts learned. The average music class time is one hour, and based on the class size, this is not enough time to spend quality time with individual students in a classroom setting. Therefore, as a band director or music teacher, you must devise a plan for your students to continue improving their craft outside of the formal rehearsal or classroom time. A number of things can be done to ensure that this happens. Give students homework, recommend that they get a private tutor, ensure that they attend workshops and master classes, and encourage them to attend band camp. Also, invite guest artists or clinicians to work with your band.

Homework

Homework is designed for students to spend time practicing and reinforcing new concepts learned in the previous class. It also serves as a means for students to practice repetition of materials already learned in order to build and improve muscle memory. Muscle memory results from doing something over and over until you do not have to think about the process involved. This is why it is important for students to learn to play a rhythm or melody accurately the first time. If they practice playing the wrong rhythm or the wrong melody in a piece of music, it will be difficult for them to play the right rhythm or melody until they have unlearned playing it the old way.

As mentioned in the previous chapter, students should be given homework at the end of each class. In some instances, you can give the entire class a particular piece of homework, such as everyone learning to play the 12 major scales; however, you will need to give additional work to the more advanced students who learn quickly or who can play their scales already. For example, these students can begin working on their minor scales. Ideally, the homework should be specific to each student. Unlike most subjects where the entire class receives the same assignment, the band class is unique because students are playing different instruments and different parts. Even if they are playing the same instrument, for example in the case of a trombone, they may be playing a different part, such as solo, first, second, or third.

Different instruments require different techniques and abilities. For example, it may be easier for a beginner trumpet player to play C major scale starting on low C, as opposed to a beginner clarinet player, because it is more difficult for a beginner clarinet player to play note B and C over the break. On the other hand, because of the nature of the instrument, it is more difficult for a trumpet player to play a slurred passage than it is for a clarinet player. Each student or section should be given a particular bar or phrase that needs to be worked on and mastered for the next class or rehearsal.

Having students work on a small section of the music at a time will be more beneficial because they will be more inclined to do their homework, as opposed to practicing the entire piece. This will be a win-win situation for both student and band. The students will be mastering and improving new skills without having to practice for long periods, and the band sound will improve as a result.

Encourage students to keep a journal of the days and times they practice, or you can design a practice schedule so they can record the relevant information. This form would also include a space to write the material or section worked on, as well as a place for the student's parent to sign as a means of confirmation, and also to get the parents involved and thus encourage their child to remain focused, to practice, and to improve on their instrument.

Private Tutor

All instrumentalists, especially those who want to pursue a career in music or get the best result from their instrument, should seek out a private tutor to help them develop and learn all the intricacies of their particular instrument. Looking at the reasons mentioned earlier—such as classroom size and the allotted class time, and the band director's limited ability on some instruments—a private tutor would be of great advantage to the student.

I, myself, benefited tremendously from a private tutor. I was introduced to playing the clarinet in 1986 by my then band director whose principal instrument was the trumpet. I learned the basics and learned to play at an acceptable level; however, for years, I played without knowing the unique mechanics of the instrument. It was not until I went to college and studied with my clarinet professor that I began to understand the key mechanism and how the instrument was designed to be played. Knowing this, I was able to play the instrument more proficiently in terms of speed and to play intricate passages easily and smoothly.

Having said the above, it is critical that band directors or music teachers ensure that their students are receiving the correct fundamentals specific to their instrument so that correct techniques are learned from the very beginning. Over the years, I have seen students play their instrument in unconventional ways. I have seen the clarinet played upside down, the right hand on top instead of the left hand, and the mouthpiece with the reed side on the top. I have seen the trumpet played with the keys in a sideways position instead of on the top, and the trombone slide upside down with the water valve side on the top or played with the left hand.

It takes time to correct bad habits once they have been ingrained, and the student's ability to excel on their instrument to an advanced level may be hindered as a result. Therefore, during the classroom setting, continue to monitor all students in order to correct bad habits.

As band director, you can provide a list of the names and contact information of private tutors for the various instruments, and the list should include tutors that teach online and/or offline. Those offline would have to be in the general area, especially if the parent has to drive their child to and from the tutor. However, there are some tutors who are willing to commute to the student. Explain to parents the benefits of having a private tutor, such as focusing on embouchure formation, alternate and auxiliary fingering techniques, and developing a characterized sound that is unique to a specific instrument.

Include all relevant information you may have regarding the tutor, such as fee, payment plan, location, and available teaching times. Having such information beforehand may help parents to make an informed decision as to whether they would be able to meet the various obligations. Again, your band will improve as a result of your students' successes.

Workshops and Master Classes

Workshops and master classes are other ways students can learn more about their instrument or related topics from experts in the field. Encourage students to participate in as many workshops and master classes as possible, especially if the workshop or masterclass is designed specifically for their instrument. It is always good for students to have a change of scenery and to learn from professionals other than yourself. This not only reinforces concepts and strategies you have been teaching them, it also presents information in other ways or from another angle so that students may understand a concept better or grasp it more quickly.

Workshops may be more general, where there is a presenter or presenters discussing and demonstrating certain topics or techniques, and the audience may be required to participate in various ways, such as playing—as a section or as the entire group—music based on the topic being discussed. There may be a question-and-answer period at the end of the workshop or students may be allowed to ask questions during the presentation. Workshops are conducted in different ways, and they can take on many forms based on what the facilitator prefers.

I can remember that years ago my school band participated in a band workshop at the College of The Bahamas. One of the trumpet players was asked to play a particular passage and he was struggling to play it. He said that his trumpet was not working properly. The facilitator asked to see his trumpet to figure out what might be wrong. He placed his mouthpiece in the trumpet and played it with such virtuosity and speed, and in the altissimo register, that it left everyone amazed. Clearly, this was a case of a classroom sign that I once read: "A bad musician blames his instrument." I knew that this experience would be an unforgettable memory in the mind of the student trumpet player and for those of us attending the workshop.

Masterclasses, on the other hand, are more specific and tend to focus attention on the individual player. Students are usually asked to prepare a piece that they will perform for the facilitator, and then receive immediate feedback from the expert on the positive and negative aspects of their performance. Other participants in the masterclass also learn from the advice and feedback given to each other as they play and are critiqued. Sometimes the facilitator will present a standard repertoire for a particular instrument, and then discuss and demonstrate how it was intended to be played or interpreted by the composer, or according to the music period when the music was composed. The facilitator may offer best practices in terms of finger combinations and alternate positions to play certain notes in order to get the best results from the music.

Band Camp

Band camps are usually conducted right before the beginning of a new semester as a means to recruit new band members, reacquaint existing band members, and sharpen the skills of the entire group.

In addition to the recruiting strategies mentioned in chapter seven, hosting band camps can be a means of adding new members to your band. The camp should be planned well in advance so that information advertising the camp is out, if not a year prior, at least before school closes for the summer break. Therefore, parents will be able to plan their child's summer break and make provisions for them to attend the camp. As well, students transitioning from the lower grade level of the same school, or from another school, can use this opportunity to join the school band.

Band camp is a way to get students back into the flow of things after they have been away on a long summer break and away from marching band season. This is particularly beneficial for those students who are not disciplined as it relates to practicing their instrument. During the camp, they are reacquainted with their instrument, the band's operating procedures, and standard drill displays. In addition, they begin working on the new repertoire and/or the new show for the upcoming season. If you do not host a camp for your band, then consider recommending that your students attend a band camp that has a program similar to yours. Some colleges and universities host band camps especially for school students that are thinking of attending college or a university upon graduating from high school.

All of the above-mentioned strategies are ways in which your individual band members can improve their overall musical skills and consequently enhance the standard of your band.

Chapter 11:

Great Melody, Great Music

Your school's mission, goals, objectives, and type of ensembles will be heavily dictated by the repertoire you stock in your library. In this chapter, repertoire refers to all the printed music that you have used throughout the entire process of developing your students and your ensemble. This includes music for the classroom instructional period up to the actual performance music. Therefore, the repertoire will include method books, sight reading books, and sheet music for both ensemble and solo pieces.

Method Books

There is an abundance of method books that are available to you, the band director—such as Essential Elements, Standard of Excellence, Rhythm Unleashed, and First Division Band Method—that cater to a wide variety of instrumental groupings. Whatever book or books you decide to work with, ensure that a conductor's score is a part of the series. These books are excellent tools to use in the band classroom because they are arranged so that all the instruments can play together, whether in unison or, in some cases, in harmony. Also, these books typically come in a series of grade levels designed to take the student from the beginner stage to the intermediate stage or, in some cases, to the advanced stage. Some books progress at a quicker pace than others, and some can be used to complement the method books you choose to use.

The method book that you decide to go with may be influenced by your personal background and training. Sometimes, teachers use books that they have been trained with, and hence are familiar with, and that have proven to be successful over many years. In some cases, band directors may choose to compose their own method books because the options that are available do not satisfy their particular needs. For example, the books may not have a special instrument that they may be teaching, or the book may move too quickly or not quickly enough. As mentioned before, instruments have unique characteristics, and in the beginning stage, one instrument may be able to play a particular range more easily than the other. Therefore, you would have to make the necessary adjustments to compensate for what the student can play until they get over the hurdle.

My advice, if the resources are available, would be to use more than one type of method book during your rehearsal as a means to keep the interest level high and to keep the students excited, as mentioned in chapter nine.

Sight Reading Books

As mentioned in chapter nine, being an excellent sight reader is probably one of the greatest assets a musician can possess. This skill is highly sought after among students, especially when they are auditioning for scholarships to attend colleges and universities or playing for a higher chair in the band. For this reason, sight reading books for the various instruments should be a part of your music program repertoire. The band method books are not ideal for sight reading, especially for the more advanced students because generally all the instruments are playing the same rhythm and melody.

Sight reading books should be specific to the various instruments because they are unique and require a different skill set. Some instruments have a wider range than others. For example, the general range of a saxophone is two-and-one-half octaves versus a clarinet with three-and-one-half octaves. Woodwind instruments, such as flutes and oboes, are more agile and thus can play a more intricate and faster melody than a trombone or a tuba. Therefore, a melody that is a grade three for a trombone may be a grade two for a flute.

In order to become great sight readers, students must work on it during every class. Reading through new materials on a consistent basis while focusing on the details, such as time signatures, key signatures, tempo, accidentals, dynamics, and intricate rhythms, will greatly enhance their sight-reading skills. The sight-reading material should be at a notch lower than the music students are capable of playing after rehearsing.

Sheet Music

As mentioned earlier, your sheet music repertoire will reflect the type of band, orchestra, or ensemble you have. For example, if you just have an orchestra or standard jazz band, there will not be a need to have marching band arrangements. Conversely, if you only have a marching band, there will be no need for orchestral arrangements. There are many online sites where you can purchase and download sheet music. These include orchestral, concert, or marching band music and small ensemble arrangements at grade levels ranging from the beginner to the advanced stage.

You should have music of various levels as a means to motivate and challenge your students. Music that the band can play can be used as part of your repertoire for concerts and performances, and to give students a sense of accomplishment because they will be able to play a piece of music that sounds good and at a moment's notice. On the other hand, more difficult music will give students a challenge and something they can work toward; thus improving their skills and also giving them a sense of achievement once the music has been mastered.

In addition to purchasing music, as a band director, if you have not done so already, you should develop the skills of transposing, arranging, or composing music for your specific band or ensemble. This is important because your band or ensemble may be called upon to play a particular song for a school function or event that is not part of your repertoire, or you may not have the resources to purchase it, or you may not be able to find an arrangement that is appropriate for your ensemble.

Arranging the music for your band will also be a way to save funds that can be used elsewhere. In some cases, you may have to transpose a piece of music for another instrument to play because you do not have that particular instrument in your band, or the student you have may not be skilled enough to play the part. Acquiring the skills to use music software such as Finale or Sibelius would be beneficial in the event you have to transpose, arrange, or compose a piece of music for your band.

Depending on the level of your students, you may have one or two students who are capable of arranging. Allow these students to arrange music for your band, thus giving them an outlet to display their talents and improve their skills. I have had a couple of students over the years who arranged music for the school band, and their fellow band members were impressed. Having students that can arrange music is also a plus because they will be more aware of the new and trending music and will tend to focus on arranging that type of music. Hence, this can be another means of motivating students to practice because they will enjoy playing music that is popular and music that they love.

Band directors and music teachers in The Bahamas typically have to arrange their own music because the folk music that is popular for bands cannot be found online or in stores. Those that do not arrange music, or do not have the time or resources to arrange music, depend on their fellow band directors to give them a copy of their music arrangements. This can be a disadvantage because then most of the bands will be playing the exact same arrangements.

Solo Music

Solo pieces such as studies, etudes, competition, exam, and recital music, at various grade levels, should also be a part of your repertoire. Such music addresses the individual needs of your students. As students mature in their musical journey, so should the music they perform. You should give students a variety of music in different genres, and the music should be challenging, thus making them better musicians and more versatile. The more students practice music they do not know how to play, the more they progress. New and more advanced music exposes them to new keys, new notes, new rhythms, new articulations, and new dynamic levels. Advanced music will also require them to play the outer extremity of their instruments.

Students should build a portfolio with music that they can play in the event they are called upon to play a solo, whether for an exam or a recital, and especially for those preparing for an audition to enter colleges and universities. Their portfolio should have a standard repertoire that is specific to their instrument. The music should be varied and thus demonstrate the ability and versatility of the student to play in various genres and styles of music. They should have music with accompaniment to demonstrate their ability to play with someone and music that is unaccompanied to show that they can play in tone by themselves without the support, in terms of chord and pitch, of the accompanying instrument.

Having access to a library with all the relevant method and sight-reading books, band arrangements, and solo pieces is essential to your band or music program. A diverse and up-to-date repertoire will help you to maintain interest among your band members and motivate them and others to come to band practice or join your music program.

Chapter 12:

Lights On, Lights Off

Center stage is the end goal for both you and your music students. Hours of practicing goes into the preparation of your students and your various ensembles to perform. Performing may include anything from playing in the classroom to playing in a concert hall. Whatever the performance, students should be conditioned and prepared to perform at their very best at all times—in the classroom environment and in recitals, auditions, exams, concerts, and competitions.

Performing in the Classroom

Depending on your job description, center stage for some may be the classroom. You may be teaching a music appreciation class where students learn an instrument as part of the class requirement, and the only place and time they will perform is during class. Students in your regular band class may be required to perform a piece at the end of a unit. Some method books have a solo piece that covers all the new notes and rhythms learned in class at a particular point in the book. Depending on the level of the class, the solo piece may be the same for everyone or specific to the various instruments. Such performances would usually be done at the classroom level. Students may be tested as a section, or individually, on their ability to play at a particular level thus far.

You may be teaching in a special school where learning an instrument is for therapeutic purposes only. Therefore, students would only play their instruments during class time, most likely in a group setting, such as a drum circle or a percussion ensemble. When I was in college, there was a music course for primary school teachers that required them to learn just the foundation of music. Learning how to play the recorder was a part of this course because it was an introductory instrument for learning melody, an introductory band instrument, and inexpensive. The purpose for this course was to equip primary teachers with the basic music skills so they would be able to teach at least the foundation in the absence of a trained music teacher. The individuals in this class were required to play their recorder in class only.

In all of the above scenarios, performance is confined to the classroom where students will play only in the presence of their classmates.

Recital Performance

Playing in a recital is no small feat. This can be a nerve wracking and stressful time for your students. The best way to prepare students for the stage is to ensure that they know their piece well enough so as not to have to rely on the music. The ultimate goal is to get them to play their entire piece from memory. In this way, you will know and your student will know that they have the music down pat.

Recitals are designed to place students at center stage on an individual level, and regular recitals should be an integral part of your music program. As students develop, they should perform in recitals in order for their family and friends to see and hear their progress. Recitals also help students to build self-confidence and self-esteem in both their playing and their personal lives. Playing in a recital forces a student to learn their music and to stand on their own two feet, as there will be no one for them to lean on.

They will be at center stage with all eyes on them.

Another way you can use a recital is to grade your students for their final exam. Students may be graded throughout the term at various intervals on specific assignments as their term grade, but a recital brings everything together. You can grade students on performance etiquette, such as holding instruments correctly while entering and leaving the stage and taking a bow before and after their performance, thus acknowledging the audience and acknowledging the accompanist as the case may be. You can also grade the playing of their instrument on the various aspects of a performance, such as tone quality, correct rhythm, style interpretation, dynamics, tempo, and phrasing.

Encouraging your students to play in recitals regularly is also the building block for learning standard repertoire specific to their instruments. This allows them to build a portfolio that will assist them in the auditioning process for music scholarships upon graduating from high school. Some colleges and universities provide a list of standard pieces to be played for the audition, while others give students the option to choose their own piece. Playing scales and sight reading is also an integral part of the auditioning process. Since the auditioning process and requirements vary from institution to institution, early research is important. A student who is well prepared will be successful in the audition.

Exam Performances

Music exams of the various grade levels are provided by The Associated Board of the Royal Schools of Music and Trinity College London at centers around the world. These exams are both practical and theory based, and are a great source for measuring your students' capabilities as they progress from one grade level to the next. These practical exams test the ability of students to play various styles of music, their sight-reading skills, and their ability to play scales; and there is also an aural component to the exam.

Once a grade level has been achieved, students are given a certificate that shows they have the capability to perform at that level.

Students that have these certificates have an advantage over their counterparts in a number of instances. I have seen students in The Bahamas who applied for summer employment at the various government agencies receive a higher rate of pay because they had a Royal School of Music certificate. In terms of applying for jobs such as in the armed forces that have a band section, students with Royal School of Music certificates are considered over those without. These certificates also serve as a prerequisite to enter the music program at The University of The Bahamas and other colleges and universities around the world where these exams are held.

Concert Performances

While recitals are to showcase the individual student, concerts are designed to place the band or ensemble at center stage and show the ability of the group to perform as a unit. You should schedule at least two band concerts in the school year. The concert shows the final result of the repertoire that you have been working on the whole semester. Concerts can take on many forms and serve many functions. For example, you can use your concert as a fundraiser, as a band recital, to help celebrate a holiday, or as part of an overall school production that includes music, dance, and drama.

Using your band concert as a means to generate funds requires promoting the concert in order for the tickets to be sold. This requires a fund-raising committee, as mentioned in chapter five, to organize all the particulars, such as designing and printing the tickets and flyers, distributing the tickets and collecting the funds, organizing the venue, and providing refreshments. All of this should be done by a committee, thus freeing you to focus on preparing the band to produce an excellent performance that people will be paying to see.

Your band concert is a means to showcase the progress of your band and to highlight the pieces the band has been working on throughout the semester. This can be an avenue for students, teachers, friends, and families to come and enjoy an afternoon or evening of music across many genres. The concert can be an outdoor event where band members can dress in pastel colors and persons can sit on the lawn in a relaxed picnic setting listening to light-hearted music; or it can be an indoor and more formal event where band members dress in formal attire and perform classical or more serious music. In any event, the band will be at center stage displaying the skills of its members.

Putting on a concert during special holidays such as Easter and Christmas will also be a great way to highlight your band and to help your school and the community celebrate the meaning of the seasons in a special way. Your band will set the mood and perform music that is suitable for the holiday. Hence, the band will have to learn a repertoire that is relevant and that encompasses the various attributes that give the season its meaning.

At the high school where I taught music, the principal organized an event called Departmental Day. This was a day when all of the departments in the school had approximately half an hour to showcase various concepts their students had learned during the semester. At one of these events, the Music and the Art Departments came together and did a presentation. The band played accompanying music while the dancers performed and the art students did splash painting and sculpturing on stage. I found this to be a very effective way to enhance the concert and make it different and more exciting.

Similar to this is an annual event held at The University of The Bahamas called Color of Harmony where the art and music students get together and put on a production to showcase students' talent and to honor an influential person who has made an invaluable contribution to the arts.

Competition Performances

Entering your band or ensemble in competitions is another way to develop your band as a whole. Students tend to be more motivated to practice because they have something to look forward to and because they are naturally competitive and love to win. During competitions, your band will be judged, critiqued, and given feedback that can contribute to the improvement of the band. You can then share the feedback with your band members and work on the areas of concern, thus helping the band to perform better at future competitions and performances.

It would also be a good idea to obtain video copies of your band's performances during competitions so they can watch it as part of the feedback and discussion period. Purchasing a professional camera for the band to be used in circumstances such as this would be even more beneficial to the band. You will not always be able to secure a recording of the band performance, and even if you do, it may not be in a timely manner. A professional camera can also be used to take quality pictures and create demo presentations to advertise your band for promotion purposes.

If a professional camera is not available, you can also use your cell phone to make video recordings. I often use my cell phone to record my band, especially to show individuals who are not doing what they are supposed to be doing. For example, I recorded a percussionist madly chewing gum during a performance while standing directly in the front of an audience. He chewed for the entire performance.

Chapter 13:

No Team, No Win

We often hear phrases like, "team work makes the dream work," "no man is an island," "it takes a village to raise a child," "many hands make light work," and "two heads are better than one" to name just a few—all of which suggest that a good team is essential to achieving your goals and objectives. This works in all aspects of society, and being a band director or music teacher is no exception. As a band director, your team consists of the principal, staff, student leaders, parents, and volunteers.

The Principal

The principal of your school should be a member of your team, if only to provide moral support. As discussed in chapter four, your goals and objectives complement the vision of the principal; and the principal has the final say in all of the decisions that may affect the growth and success of your music program. Making the principal aware of your plans, how they contribute to the goals of the school, and the deadlines to accomplish them will encourage the principal to be more expedient in decision-making.

I would like to remind you that the principal has responsibility for the entire school and has to make decisions on a daily basis as to which department or physical plant aspect of the school he or she will spend the available funds on. Every department believes that their concerns are more important and must be dealt with urgently. In my present role as an administrator, one of my job descriptions is the physical plant. As I walk around the school documenting for the summer scope of work, every teacher in every classroom has a concern that needs to be addressed, for example: ceiling tile missing, air conditioner needed, lights and fans not coming on, roof leaking, wall cracking, and window operators broken.

Safety comes first. In this regard, all of the concerns dealing with the safety aspect of the school, such as exposed wires or doors that may be falling off the hinges must be dealt with first. Next, the basic needs must be taken care of, such as proper lighting, sufficient furniture, and proper ventilation. Last, all of the wishes and concerns of the various departments will be dealt with in order of priority and availability of funds, as the principal sees fit.

I have worked with principals who worked closely with the music program and knew the urgency of getting things done, and therefore signed checks in a timely fashion. On the other hand, I have worked with principals who told me to spend personal funds to purchase what was needed and that I would be reimbursed. In doing it this way, I sometimes waited a long time for that school check.

Staff Members

You will become your teachers' teacher, and your students will become your teachers. This all boils down to building relationships. The relationships you have built during your journey thus far can assist you in building your support team. Teaching in a new school may place you in a position to cross paths with and impart knowledge and skills to your teachers and to have your students impart their knowledge to you. Living in a county, a state, or a small country, like The Bahamas, will almost guarantee you the above experience.

I have been placed in such a position on a number of occasions. The first teaching position I got as a trained teacher was in a high school, and I became a colleague of Mrs. Dorsette, my high school biology teacher. She was one of my favorite teachers in high school, and I was even able to show her my biology notebook from when I was in her class. Although we were not teaching the same subject, our paths crossed when we worked on school-related functions. I was then able to impart some of my knowledge and skills to her for the betterment of the project.

In another instance, I became a colleague of my college professor, now deceased, Mrs. Audrey Dean Wright, when I began working as a part-time lecturer at the College of the Bahamas, now the University of he Bahamas. I felt honored that Mrs. Wright sought my professional help on a number of occasions, and I was able to give her sound advice. On the other hand, some of my former students became my colleagues and I was able to seek advice from them that was beneficial to me. Therefore, during your quest for a support team, know that you can sometimes rely on relationships that have already been built.

The staff members, consisting of teachers and support staff, are a vital part of your team. Teachers will be very useful when it comes to assisting your band members. They can assist in ensuring that the students are focused and well-rounded individuals, hence, keeping up with their academics and maintaining an acceptable grade point average. This is important, especially for students who are aspiring to go to colleges or universities. You can have a team of teachers that organize extra classes for music students that are falling behind, and for those that are taking exams such as PSATs and SATs. Students must be made aware that being able to play their instrument at a high standard will not, in itself, get them a scholarship or get them into college or a university. They must have the academics to go with it.

Teachers who are part of your team generally know the band members and will be able to keep them in line with reference to discipline problems. Students tend to conduct themselves accordingly, especially when they are in the presence of teachers who know their face and more importantly, their name. When I was in the classroom, on many occasions, teachers would bring a band student to me for discipline problems and/or for not completing their assignments. On every occasion, I was able to talk to the student and get better results. Some students display different behavior when they are in band or music class than they do in another subject area.

I have dealt with a number of student-athletes for misbehaving or for being defiant towards myself or other teachers. Once I take them to their coach, they get a good tongue lashing and are dealt with severely. Almost all of them change their behavior, or at least they do for the time they are in my presence. Teachers are very important allies to help curb bad behavior.

It is important to check up on your students and make sure that they are attending school regularly and are going to their other subject classes. Over the years, I have had students who only attended school during days that they had band classes, and even on those days, they would not attend their other classes. These students, for the most part, were academically challenged, and playing an instrument was a skill that helped to build their self-esteem. Monitoring these students with the assistance of teachers will keep them focused and out of trouble.

Support staff include all the individuals on staff other than the teachers, namely security officers, secretaries, janitors, and the yardmen. Each of them can assist the band director in their own unique way. Security officers can provide a safe environment for your band members, especially during practices outside of regular school hours. They can keep a watchful eye on the outside perimeter of your practice area and serve as a deterrence to trespassers. They can travel with the band on field trips and performances to add extra protection of personnel and to keep a watchful eye over the band instruments and equipment.

On a number of occasions during my time in the classroom, security officers would bring an instrument to me and say that they had found it somewhere outside while they were doing their rounds of the school. Students may have carelessly left their instrument outside after the completion of a rehearsal or while traversing the campus.

As for the secretaries, they can assist with the timely drafting and completion of letters and student consent forms that need to get distributed quickly. They can do all the necessary calling in terms of getting quotes, communicating with parents and sponsors, and taking care of the relevant performance details. This will take pressure off you, so you can spend less time doing administrative work and more time on the technical aspects of your band.

Janitors and the yardmen are also important to your team because these are the persons responsible for cleaning and preparing your classrooms and the outside environment so you can have a safe and sanitized place to practice. The band room can become an unhealthy environment as students playing wind instruments are constantly letting condensation out of their instruments. Sometimes the condensation may find its way to the floor and can be unsafe in two regards.

First, it can cause someone to slip if they happen to step in it, and second, being on the ground, it can bring germs into the environment. Therefore, the janitor or janitress must clean the band room regularly to avoid accidents or potential spreading of disease. Likewise, the yardmen can make sure that the lawn on the practice field is properly groomed and that there are no objects lying around, such as sticks and stones that can cause a student to trip during marching practice.

Student Leaders

Student leaders are like the band director's right hand, because unlike the other team members, they know the ins and outs of the band's daily operating procedure. For example, the student leaders should be capable of running the band in the absence of the director. I recall a baccalaureate service—a major event in the life of the high school in which I taught—that I was unable to attend. The school's band was scheduled to perform during the service, so I left the band captain in charge of the band under the supervision of one of the teachers.

The students did such an awesome job that the priest turned over the money collected during the offering to the band. This had never happened to me in my tenure as band director at that school. It illustrates the capabilities of students when they are trained and you give them an opportunity to serve in a leadership position.

As a band director, your student leaders can consist of the following positions: Drum major, band captain, assistant band captain, section leaders for the various instruments, and librarian. A good idea may be to allow students to wear name tags identifying that they are student leaders of the band. This makes them feel special and gives them a sense of pride. Also, other students will be looking forward to being in those positions at some point. These positions can increase or decrease in numbers depending on the size of your band or ensemble. For example, a drum major position is only required if you have a marching band at your school; and if you have a large marching band, you may need more than one drum major.

Student leaders should be competent on their various instruments, possess leadership skills, have a positive attitude, be consistent, follow the rules and regulations of the school and the band, and represent the band director and the school at the highest level. For example, a student could be the best player on his or her instrument but not be a suitable section leader because he or she is not consistent about coming to band rehearsals or has a bad attitude. In some cases, you may have to appoint the "lesser of two evils," or go without a section leader until you can find a good fit.

Sometimes you may have to place a specific instrument type under the section leader of another instrument type that belongs to the same family of instruments. For example, you may have to place the saxophones and clarinets under one section leader, thus making this student section leader for the single reed instruments.

The band librarian will be responsible for organizing a team to make sure that all sheet music is distributed or placed in folders, collected, and filed away in the appropriate place and at the appropriate time. The librarian will ensure that individuals are accountable for their folder and its contents. Signing a form designed for such a purpose will indicate that they have received the same. Students who lose their music will be asked to pay for a replacement. Hence, knowing the cost of the folders and the sheet music is important.

Parents

All music programs should have a parent support group or band parent association of some kind. A triangle is sometimes used to show the components of a successful education system, and the sides include the school, the child, and the parent. Therefore, parents are one of the most important equations in the development and sustainability of your music program. While this is ideal, receiving full support from parents is a task within itself. Depending on the country, location, and type of school—whether public or private, will determine the percentage of parents' support that you receive.

From my experience and observation over the years, private schools tend to receive overwhelming parent support, while the public schools struggle to get parents to support their children. I have worked in band programs where I have never seen some of the band members' parents. They never attended a fundraiser, concert, recital, or performance. I can remember one particular case where we were taking a youth band on an international trip and some individuals were travelling for the first time. The parents of the children were required to attend a meeting to sign insurance and consent forms in order for their child to go on the trip. I had to literally take a young girl home in order for a parent to sign her forms because her parent did not show up to the meeting.

Nonetheless, the parents that you have as a part of your support team tend to make up for the delinquent parents. These parents can take much of the burden off the band director, thus giving him more time to work on the band itself. Parents can spearhead fundraisers, plan trips, encourage more parents to get involved with the program, and use their diverse backgrounds and professions to accomplish many tasks that need to be done.

You would be surprised to know the wealth of knowledge, connection, and influence of your students' parents. I have had parents who were able to secure funds from private citizens to sponsor the band members' international trip; parents who were able to provide professional catering services for band special events; and a parent who was able to get a political figurehead to attend a band event after several other attempts had been made.

Supportive parents are also directly correlated to supportive students. These students are usually consistent about coming to rehearsals, are well behaved, attend the performances, and practice their instrument regularly.

Parents are also good chaperones when it comes to traveling and other events, such as band socials, field trips, and special performances. Parents at band performances are also a plus because they are the band's biggest fans and supporters, and watching over the students will be their primary focus.

Also, other parents will be more inclined to allow their child to participate in band events if they know that other individuals with the same interest as them will be at the event. That interest is to ensure that their child is safe, secure, and well taken cared of. Again, when more parents are attending, the band director will be able to concentrate on the more technical aspects of the band.

Volunteers

Volunteers can be anyone from the community, whether private or corporate, who has a mandate to give back to nonprofit organizations or who just loves music and/or loves to see young children engaged in positive activities. Over the years, I have had former students and other musician acquaintances give up their time to work with the school band on various aspects, whether speaking about college, teaching a new piece of music, or organizing a new marching display.

While volunteers can contribute either time or finances, many persons support the band program more on a financial level in terms of providing what is needed to operate on a daily basis. In this regard, you should always have a list of instruments and equipment that are needed, along with prices, in the event a sponsor asks for it. The school where I taught had a Lodge Hall situated across the street from the school, and the Lodge Hall decided to partner with the school. I was asked for the type of instruments that were needed and I told them. They bought wind instruments for the band including clarinets, saxophones, and trumpets.

Another time, a business establishment in the community got the school band to perform at their cultural event and in turn gave the band a monetary donation to purchase instruments. Churches in the community who had fairs also got the school band to play and then gave a monetary donation. A hotel in the community adopted my school, and as a result we were able to rent their ballroom for special events at a discounted price.

In another instance, a private citizen who loved the band's music made his contribution by encouraging his contacts to donate a grand piano and an electric keyboard. Also, on occasion, individuals would donate an instrument that they had lying around the house, something that they used to play or that they had bought for their child and it was no longer being used. Generally, volunteers will tend to assist you and help promote your program when they notice that you have your students' best interest at heart and are working with what you have and genuinely trying to propel your program forward.

Maintaining the resources that you have is essential to sustaining the inventory discussed in chapter five. Teaching proper handling and care of instruments, upkeep of equipment, and proper storage will enable you to benefit from the total lifespan of instruments and equipment, and even beyond.

Many schools that I know of have cupboards or a storage room filled with musical instruments that are not working. Some of these instruments are damaged and can only be used for spare parts. On the other hand, some of the instruments are a simple fix, such as a broken trumpet guide that is preventing the valve from going up and down, or a missing saxophone pad that is preventing notes from being played. Being able to fix these instruments will add any number of working instruments to your inventory, thus allowing more students to participate in class and/or play in your band.

Instrument Repair

As a band teacher, if you have not yet done so, one of the continuing education classes that you should take is an instrument repair course, if only for the basics. Knowing how to do minor repairs and adjustment to your students' instruments is an asset that will save you both time and money. You would probably appreciate this idea even more if there was an instrument malfunction right before an important performance and it happened to be one of your solo players. Most of the time it will be a simple fix, even if only temporary, but you have to be knowledgeable about troubleshooting and fixing minor problems. I have done the instrument repair course at VanderCook College of Music, which gave me the skills to identify problems and repair instruments, thus saving my program thousands of dollars every year.

The youth band program that I work with currently consists of children starting at age seven, and at every band practice there are a couple of instruments that need to be repaired on the spot. The basic problems are stuck mouthpieces, loose or weak springs, bent keys, missing pads, and unaligned trumpet guide. Most of these problems exist because of improper handling and care of the instruments. Another problem that contributes to the constant malfunction of these instruments is the fact that the majority of parents buy inferior instruments for their child or children. You will find that knowing how to do basic instrument repair is a great asset; it will save you a lot of stress and time when it comes to maneuvering around these many minor and major occurrences.

Proper Handling & Care

Teaching students how to assemble and disassemble their instruments when beginning their classes is essential in order to prevent problems in the future. I spend a considerable amount of time teaching proper handling of instruments during the first few classes until I can see that the students are doing it right. Once it becomes a habit, you will not have to worry about it; you will just have to give occasional reminders if you see something going awry.

If the students are not taught the right way, they will do all kinds of weird things. I had a little girl whose mother had bought her a clarinet, and I asked her if she had practiced the instrument yet and she said yes. So, I enquired as to how she had assembled the instrument and if she had used the cork grease. She said yes, and when I asked where she had applied the cork grease, she said that she had put it on her lip! She thought that the cork grease was to be applied to the lip before playing because it looked like Chapstick. Another student's trumpet needed oiling and he used cooking oil on the valves, thus leaving the trumpet greasy all over and smelling like a kitchen.

Most students playing the clarinet, if they are not taught the right way to assemble the instrument, will bend the bridge key. I have found this to be one of the most common problems in all the bands that I have worked with over the years. Another problem with reference to the woodwind instruments is not applying cork grease to the cork joints before assembling the instrument. This results in a dry fit that quite often causes the cork to peel off. Applying cork grease to the cork joints also gives the joints a better seal.

A common occurrence as it relates to brass instruments is a loose brace as a result of stuck mouthpieces. Students who have not been taught to insert their mouthpiece correctly tend to get it stuck by hitting the mouthpiece in with their hand or knocking it against another object. Once the mouthpiece gets stuck, the student or their parent try to take the mouthpiece out with a pair of pliers, thus wringing the lead pipe and consequently breaking the brace. Another cause for the mouthpiece getting stuck is as a result of students dropping their mouthpiece and bending the end of the shank. The shank, which is supposed to be round in shape is then square, and inserting a square shank into a round mouthpiece receiver results in it getting stuck.

Students who play valve instruments sometimes take the valves out of their instrument and then mix up the order in which they should be replaced. As a result, they will not be able to play their instrument. The students have to be taught that the valves all have numbers on the body that have to match up with the appropriate cylinder. I often tell students that if something goes wrong with their instrument, they should not experiment, but rather bring it to me and I will show them what to do to fix the problem. It is important not to leave students on their own until they know how to assemble and disassemble their instruments correctly, especially in the beginning stage.

Students should also be taught not to sit on instrument cases, especially the soft ones. Sitting on an instrument case not only damages the case but more importantly, the instrument. The case is designed to secure the instrument with a tight fit. Sitting on a case adds undue pressure to the case, and that pressure is transferred to the instrument, thus bending a post or key out of alignment.

Another point: Students, while in practice mode, should secure their instrument on an instrument stand when they are not playing it. Instruments lying around on the floor, chair, or table are accidents waiting to happen—for both students and instruments. Once an instrument falls, you can guarantee that something will be bent or moved out of alignment. It takes a very small fraction of movement for instruments to leak and to not play correctly due to misalignment.

I often see students walking on the street or walking to school with their instrument out of the case. When asked why they do not have their instrument in its case, they give excuses such as the case is too heavy to walk with or to catch the bus with, or the case is damaged in one way or the other. Some of them even travel with their instrument in their school bag. All of this contributes to the instrument's malfunction because during their travels they are resting the instrument down and/or hitting it against other objects without even realizing it.

In the event of damaged instruments cases, there can be temporary fixes until another one is secured. You can allow students to use the case of an instrument that is damaged and not being utilized. Also, students can use a belt, strap, and buckle or Velcro to secure cases that are not closing due to broken zippers and latches.

Instruct students *not* to use their instrument as a weapon, such as wielding it around and attempting to hit other students with it. There should be no horseplay of any sort in the band room in order to avoid potential accidents involving instruments and also equipment such as protruding cases and music and instrument stands.

The students should be taught to clean their instrument daily after playing it, and a complete overhaul should be done by a qualified person at the specified time. The percussion section should have regular cleaning sessions of their drums, cymbals, and other equipment in order to eliminate corrosion, keep moving parts working freely, and keep a good shine on the surfaces.

Instrument Storage

Proper storage of instruments and equipment is essential to their upkeep. Instruments should be stored in their proper case when not in use and not transported without their specific case. This is probably the number one reason why large instruments like tubas, sousaphones, and baritones are full of dents. From my experience, sousaphones either do not have proper working cases to secure them or the cases are too large to transport. Therefore, they are transported without the cases in order for them to fit into vehicles such as small cars in the absence of proper transportation.

At the school where I first started teaching, there were a few cupboards where the instruments were stored, and they were designed to hold only the small instruments. The larger instruments, such as baritones, tenor saxes, tubas, and trombones were kept directly on the ground. As I began to accumulate more instruments, they were beginning to pile up on each other. Therefore, I requested some materials from the school and used one of the skillful Carpentry and Joinery students to help me build shelves so I was able to store instruments on various levels and not have them sitting directly on the ground. As band director, you must find solutions to make your work better and more organized, thus making you more efficient in carrying out your job. If you cannot do the work yourself, then use the available resources that are right there in your school, namely talented students and teachers who do not mind assisting you to build your program.

Equipment and resources such as band folders, method books, and music stands should be secured properly when not in use. Encourage students to use the music stands only for holding music books and folders and not to rest their instruments or body weight on the stands. Under no circumstances should this be done as it will weaken the stands, especially the non-heavy-duty stands. Students should sit in the chairs the way they were designed to be used. Keep the instrument cases stored in the storage room or a designated area during rehearsals and classes so as to avoid accidents like students tripping over them, thus hurting themselves as well as damaging the instrument cases.

Always try to take good care of what you have, because you may not know when and where the next set of funds will be coming from. You should not have the right to complain of lack of funding for instruments and equipment if you are not taking care of what you already have. A lack of certain instruments will place you at a disadvantage in terms of the sound of your band and in terms of engaging as many students in your class as possible. Maintaining a safe, clean environment is not only helpful for sustaining your instruments and equipment; it is also conducive to learning.

Chapter 15:
Motivated, Dedicated

In the education system, the students are our customers. Therefore, we should serve them to the best of our abilities. We should do our best to ensure that they get a quality education, thus helping them to become well-rounded individuals. Students should be able to use the lessons learned to enhance themselves and make a positive impact in their communities, their country, and the world. Students in your music program are some of the hardest working students in the school because they are always out there performing and being ambassadors for their school.

I often remind my school's administration team that the music students deserve to be rewarded and celebrated, because unlike the other students, they serve the school from the first day of school to the last day of school. As an example, my band students performed for the first general assembly, thus officially opening the school year, and the most important event of the school—the graduation ceremony—thus closing the school year. At those events, band students were the first individuals to arrive because they had to set up the band equipment, and the last to leave because they had to break down the equipment and then take it all back to the school or secure it in the band room.

School Marketing

Along with the sporting program, the music program is essential in the marketing of your school. These are the students who are always out there in public and who are captured in the media representing the school in a positive light. They serve as public relations for your school because they carry the school's banner, wear the school's uniform, and display the school's logo and colors. Your school's name is highlighted every time your team plays or your band performs.

When I taught in a high school, I often had students in the primary school say that they wanted to come to my school after they had heard the high school band perform at their school's function or at some other event. I also had parents come to me and say that they wanted their child to attend my school because they saw that the school had a great band and a great music program. My school band was also asked to perform at numerous community engagements as a result of people seeing and hearing the band perform, thus bringing positive reviews to the school.

I often asked the individuals who were requesting that the school band perform at a particular event what their reason was for requesting us, and they usually said they had heard that we were the best school band for their particular event.

Due to the above-mentioned reasons, it is important to show appreciation to the music students and to keep them motivated with various initiatives, such as pizza parties, an award system, and celebrations. And it is important to ask them what their favorite ways of celebrating would be.

Pizza Party

An inexpensive way to show appreciation and motivate students to continue working hard is to have pizza parties. The number of individuals in your band will determine the amount of pizza you need to order. An average would be two or three slices of pizza per student, and you will be able to take advantage of specials and discounts for ordering a large number of pizzas. It will also be a good idea to preorder your pizzas so they will be ready in time because you are working with limited time. Students love the camaraderie, and it will save them having to purchase or bring lunch for that particular day.

Every other month, especially after a number of performances, I would request funds from the school in order to have a pizza party for the band students. This was usually not a problem because the money often came from donations received by the band as a result of performances. And some individuals would sponsor a pizza party as a contribution to the band for performing at their event. A pizza party does not have to take away instructional time from the students because it can be held during the lunch period. Only the music students that have been performing during the immediate past performances are allowed to partake and they are given permission to play dance music and let their hair down for the hour. This not only motivates the band members but also serves as motivation for those students not in the band. They want to join the band because they feel like they are missing out on the fun.

Awards Banquet

An award system we used in the high school where I taught was introduced by my former Head of Department, now retired, Mrs. Marjorie Knowles. It was called "Evening with the Stars." This was an award recital dinner banquet, primarily to showcase and celebrate the seniors (grade 12) of the music program, with their teachers, family, and friends in attendance. This was an exciting time for the students because they had an opportunity to show off their formal wear and elaborate hairstyles. The students would perform solo pieces during dinner, and afterwards receive certificates, plaques, and trophies based on their accomplishments and performance throughout their tenure at the school.

A souvenir booklet was also produced, including a picture and biography of each of the students being celebrated, as well as congratulatory ads. Students in grade 10 and 11 were the ushers and servers for the event. This gave them and other music students inspiration as they had something to look forward to during their senior year.

Student Appreciation Assembly

Music students were also included in my school's annual celebrations rewarding students from the various academic and sporting teams that had represented the school throughout the school year. They were entertained, recognized, and given certificates at a special assembly, and then treated to a lunch prepared at the school or taken to a buffet via buses at one of the hotel restaurants on the island. At the school, students were also treated to a dance, which they seem to love most of all.

Students were also shown appreciation throughout the year by being given free tickets to concerts and other events. They also received small tokens such as bags, caps, and meal vouchers for popular fast food restaurants throughout the island.

Beach Picnic or Pool Party

Another fun activity you can use to reward your music students is to have a beach picnic or a pool party. However, unless you have the manpower, I would reserve such events for a smaller grouping. Because of the fact that water is involved, organizing an event such as this requires a lot more chaperones, including specialized chaperones. The teacher-to-student ratio must increase when students are around water. Safety is paramount; therefore, you must have lifeguards and additional persons trained in CPR. Also, strict rules and guidelines governing students' behavior in and out the water must be adhered to. For example, students should operate on a buddy system while in the water and not stray away from the group or go out in the deep, especially if they are non-swimmers. A beach picnic can be an enjoyable occasion for students as long as all of the safety mechanisms are in place.

While on a band trip in the USA, we allowed the students to go in the pool. One of the girls appeared to have a cramp because she was unable to move and had to be assisted out of the pool. Nobody knew what had happened; however, she claimed that someone had hit her while in the pool. Being the person in charge, I instructed the hotel to call an ambulance in order to take the student to the hospital as a safety precaution. She was examined and turned out to be fine. At the time of the incident, students were playing and jumping in the pool, even though they were instructed not to do so. I, along with a parent, was supervising the students. However, more adult supervision would have been beneficial so as to monitor all students at all times and to stop them immediately if they indulged in rough play.

What was different is that we normally did not allow students to go in the pool when we travelled abroad so as to avoid occurrences such as the one mentioned above. In this case, students were begging to go in the pool, and the very time we relaxed our "rule" something happened.

Field Trips

Field trips can be fun experiences for students, as there are numerous types of activities that can be planned. They can participate in a scavenger hunt throughout a section of your city or town or a specific historical sight. They can spend the day at the movie or entertainment center, or they can go on an organized sightseeing tour. They can also spend the day at a theme park or roller-skating rink or even travel to another state or country.

There are numerous ways you can reward your students, and it is a good idea to get feedback from your students as to what they might love to do as a group. The idea is to keep them motivated and to ensure that they feel appreciated for the contribution they are making to their school. Students know when they are appreciated and they also know when they are overdue for a treat—at which point they usually verbalize it. Students are not to be exploited and should be treated fairly and with respect at all times, because they are the reason that the school exists, and if there are no students, there will be no teachers.

Conclusion

Being the new band director or music teacher in a school can be a challenging but also very rewarding experience. If you follow the advice laid out in this book, you will have great information based on my 30-plus years of experience working with bands and young people as well as my suggestions from other "people's" experiences. At the very least, you will have a foundation or a starting point to build upon. As you progress, take on new initiatives, and mature as a new teacher, this information is here to guide you through the process. Take the information and adapt it to your unique situation as you develop a brand of your own.

Continue to experiment and tweak the various concepts outlined in this book so that you have more tools in your toolbox. There is no one solution to any situation because every personality is different, and you may encounter students with personalities you have never seen before. Remember that students are your *customers* and it is your job to find creative ways to assist them and support them. One of my colleagues in school always likes to say, "There is never a dull moment." This is true for the very fact that every student is different, and every school year is different because there are new students, and in some instances, new teachers and/or a new principal.

I am always willing to give advice whenever I can affect positive change. Thus, contact me with questions or reference information in the book where you may need further clarification.

Appendices

Appendix 1: Parental Consent Form

SCHOOL NAME:
ADDRESS:
TELEPHONE:
EMAIL:

Wednesday, 3 April 2019
Dear Parent/Guardian,
The students of the school's band will be visiting the
_______________________________ Friday, 5 April 2019 at 9:00 a.m. to
perform for the ___________________________ event. They will be
accompanied by Mr./Mrs. _______________________________, teacher(s)
from the school.
Transportation will be provided from the school to the
_______________________________ and back to the school.
Please complete the consent form below and return it on or before
Friday, 5 April 2019.
Thank you for your cooperation.
Sincerely,

____

Teacher

____

Principal

PARENTAL CONSENT FORM

(Please tick as appropriate, then sign and return)

I give consent ☐   I do not give consent ☐
For my child to attend the _______________________________ Friday, 3 April
2019 at 9:00 a.m.

Student's Name: _______________________________ Grade: _______

Please tick one that applies:
School Insurance ☐   Personal Insurance (provide proof) ☐
No Insurance: I claim full responsibility for any incident that might occur. ☐

Parent's/Guardian's Name (PRINT)

____

Parent's/Guardian's Signature: _______________________________ Date: _______

Appendix 2: Instrument Inventory Sheet

SCHOOL NAME:
ADDRESS:
TELEPHONE:
EMAIL:

Date: _____________________   Page: _______ of _________

INVENTORY SHEET

#	INSTRUMENT	MAKE/ MODEL	SERIAL NUMBER	DATE RECEIVED	NEW/GOOD/ NEED REPAIR/ DAMAGE	CASE YES/NO

Appendix 3: Equipment Inventory Sheet

SCHOOL NAME:
ADDRESS:
TELEPHONE:
EMAIL:

Date: _____________________ Page: _______ of __________

INVENTORY SHEET

#	EQUIPMENT	MAKE/ MODEL	SERIAL NUMBER	DATE RECEIVED	NEW/GOOD/ NEED REPAIR/ DAMAGE	

Appendix 4: Instrument Sign-Out/In Sheet

SCHOOL NAME:
ADDRESS:
TELEPHONE:
EMAIL:

INSTRUMENT SIGN OUT/IN SHEET

#	INSTRUMENT	SERIAL NUMBER	SIGN OUT	SIGN IN	DATE	PARTICULARS

Appendix 5: Music Folder Sign Out/In Sheet

SCHOOL NAME:
ADDRESS:
TELEPHONE:
EMAIL:

BAND MUSIC FOLDER SIGN OUT/IN SHEET

#	MUSIC FOLDER	STUDENT NAME	SIGN OUT	SIGN IN	DATE	PARTICULARS
1						
2						
3						
4						
5						
6						
7						
8						
9						
10						
11						
12						
13						
14						
15						
16						
17						
18						
19						
20						
21						

Appendix 6: Practice Journal

SCHOOL NAME:
ADDRESS:
TELEPHONE:
EMAIL:

STUDENT NAME_______________________________

PRACTICE JOURNAL

DATE	ASSIGNMENT	SU	M	T	W	TH	F	SAT

Appendix 7: Band Application Form

SCHOOL NAME:
ADDRESS:
TELEPHONE:
EMAIL:

BAND APPLICATION FORM

Please complete this form in **BLOCK CAPITALS** and submit it to the office.

Name: ____

     Surname   Christian Name   Middle Initial

Date of Birth _______________________________________

Place of Birth _______________________________________

Address: ____

____

____

P. O. Box: ___________ Telephone: ___________________

Email: ___________________________________Grade: ______

Choose which instrument you would like to play by choosing a first and second option.

Flute__	Trumpet__	Snare Drum__	Violin__
Oboe__	French__	Tenor Drum__	Viola__
Clarinet__	Horn__	Quads__	Cello__
Bassoon__	Mellophone__	Bass Drum__	Double Bass__
Alto Sax__	Trombone__	Cymbal__	Guitar__
Tenor Sax__	Baritone__	Mallet__	Bass Guitar__
Baritone Sax__	Tuba__	Percussion_	Other__
		Piano__	

Signature of Parent: _____________________________ Date: _________

Signature of Child: ______________________________ Date: _________

Appendix 8: Personal Information Form

SCHOOL NAME:
ADDRESS:
TELEPHONE:
EMAIL:

PERSONAL INFORMATION FORM

To be filled out by **Parent/Guardian**

Student Name: _________________________ Date of Birth: ____________

Age: ____________________ Sex: ____________

Name of Parent/Guardian: _________________Contact: _______________

<u>IN THE EVENT OF AN EMERGENCY, PLEASE NOTIFY:</u>

Name: ______________________ Relationship: _____________
Phone: ____________________________

Name: ______________________ Relationship: _____________
Phone: ____________________________

Name of Personal Physician: ______________________________

Phone: ______________________

Personal Health/Accident Insurance Carrier: __________________________
Policy: ______________________

List any medication to be taken: _________________________________

List any physical or behavioral conditions that may affect or limit full participation in activities:

____

____

____

Immunizations (Give date of last inoculation): _________________

<u>IN CASE OF EMERGENCY:</u>

I UNDERSTAND EVERY EFFORT WILL BE MADE TO CONTACT ME. IN THE EVENT I CANNOT BE REACHED, I HEREBY GIVE PERMISSION TO THE LICENSED HEALTH CARE PRACTITIONER SELECTED BY THE ADULT LEADER IN CHARGE TO SECURE PROPER TREATMENT, INCLUDING HOSPITILIZATION, ANESTHESIA, OR INJECTIONS OF MEDICATION FOR MY CHILD.

Signature of Parent/Guardian: ___________________________ Date: _________

Author's Biography

Oscar Shorn Dames

Oscar Dames is a certified teacher and is now the Senior Master at C.I. Gibson Senior High School in Nassau NP, Bahamas. He also is a part-time music lecturer at the University of The Bahamas in the School of Communication and Creative Arts. He holds an AA (Music) and a Bachelor of Education degree from the College of The Bahamas, and a Masters in Music Education from Vander-Cook College of Music in Chicago. Oscar was C.R. Walker Senior High School's Teacher of the Year 2010-2012. He was the school's band director and coordinator for the School's Junior Junkanoo program, setting a new record when the school became the only high school to win first place in three consecutives Junior Junk-anoo parades.

A big believer in culture and community building, Oscar spends much of his time teaching community bands, as he is the band director for the Nassau Village Urban Renewal Band, Assistant Director of the Royal Ambassadors Band, and the leader and founder of the Fiesta Fun Junkanoo Group. Oscar was a member of the Saxons Superstars Junkanoo Group, beating the tom-tom and bass drum before taking over the "Brass Section," and setting a new record winning five consecutive best music awards, which remains today. Oscar also plays solo clarinet and bassoon with The Bahamas Symphony Orchestra.

Oscar Dames graduated in 1988 from R.M. Bailey Senior High School with the Most Outstanding Music Award. Upon graduating, he joined the Royal Bahamas Defence Force in 1989. Oscar served for almost 14 years in the Defence Force where he was a member of the Hull Engineering Department, and he also played with and served as a training officer for the Defence Force Band. Upon transferring from the Royal Bahamas Defence Force to the Ministry of Education, Oscar enlisted in the Royal Bahamas Police Force Reserve on 17 May 2005. He is a member of the Royal Bahamas Police Force Band and serves as education instructor for the Police Reserve Band section. Oscar is also a Journeyman plumber registered with the Ministry of Works, Nassau Bahamas. He holds a second degree black belt in Judo; and he enjoys teaching, swimming, and playing music in various ensembles. To contact Oscar, please call 242-422-0593, 242-362-1609, or email Oscar@coralwave.com, oscarshorndames@gmail.com, or Oscarshorndames@hotmail.com.